UPS AND I

OF A POKER I

by

JOHN COWELL

&

STEVE WOOD

RB

Rossendale Books

Published byAmazon KDP Publishing

Published in paperback 2021
Category: Non-Fiction
Copyright John Cowell, Steve Wood © 2021
ISBN : 9798493667541

CONTENTS

ACKNOWLEDGEMENTS

Steve and I would like to thanks all the characters who volunteered to bare their souls and take part in our book.

A special thanks goes out to DarrenYates who organises many of our poker schedules. It is not an easy job to organise a game of Texas Hold'em when over forty players are involved but he makes the job look easy. The task has been even more difficult due to the Corona Virus Pandemic. This proved even more so when trying to organise the scheduled game between the ten contestants

Thanks also go out to Darren's partner, Colette, who makes the job run smoothly by organising seat changes and gathering in of chips during every competition.

Also to Procky, one of the book's characters, for running a bounty at every event to make the game even more interesting.

Thanks also to Peter and Mark who organise the smooth running of games at Read Social Club.

A special thanks to Steve's daughter in law, Jacky Hesketh and my son Craig, for painstakingly proofreading the book. Jacky also happens to be the secretary of Steve's charity, HYNDBURN STRAY DOGS IN NEED. Also a special thanks to Craig for designing the book cover.

We mustn't forget Rebecca Hanley, a young lady who courageously kept the beer flowing during difficult times having to carry trays of drinks up two flights of stairs during poker events.

We extend our gratitude to the Ighten Leigh Club for allowing us, even under difficult circumstances, to partake in our contests.

I wish to thank my cousin Vincent Walsh for publishing this book.

We'd also like to thank all the players who participate every Thursday evening at Darren's poker sessions and also those who play at Read and Simonstone Constitutional Club for all the funny tales and canny remarks they come out with during an event. Without you all ... this book would not have been possible.

Steve and I are both grateful to our wives Sue and Elsina, for bearing with us whilst we spent countless hours researching, interviewing and writing the book.

INTRODUCTION

The reason why I started to write this book is quite simple. I have lived a long interesting life and experienced many things. But, with all my worldly experience, I had never ever played poker until I was 79 years of age. I'd played Don, Cribbage, Queens and many other card games but never poker. I first played the magical game when I was in Tasmania, Australia, and I've been hooked on it ever since.

I have written ten other books which have been well received all over the world. But I had no plans to write another novel until Steve Wood, a good friend, of mine, approached me and asked if I would take on the task.

"A book about Poker," I asked, "how can I possibly write a full book about it?"

"John!" he stressed, there's millions of people all over the world who simply love this fantastic game. And it's not just the card sharps in Las Vegas ... even countries like China, India, Brazil and Australia simply love the game."

"Yeah, I'm aware of that but I don't know enough about the game to write a full book about it."

"Oh come off it John, it won't just be about the funny antidotes and all the ins and outs of the game. Ten players sit around a table and you can reflect back over their lives. You've got to admit there's a load of characters amongst poker players. And don't forget it's a great leveller ... you get people from all walks of life but, once they're sat at the table, they're all on equal terms and everyone wants to win. Also, Texas Hold'em is reckoned by many to be the ultimate poker game. Hands constantly come under rapid fire which gives a player a chance to recoup their losses or even double up on their chips. When chips are low it is often a 'do or die' situation and a build up of adrenaline drives an individual to go All In. Nothing ventured ... nothing gained. If it pays off, it creates an indescribable joyful feeling."

After our little chat he got me to thinking that it would indeed make a good story. And so, let it be written, I took on the challenge. But I only agreed to do so if Steve helped me to research different valleys and chase up on some of our chosen characters. It turned out that many of the stories were hilarious, some were serious and others poignant, but, then again ... that's for you to decide.

FOREWORD

Texas Hold'em Poker is a beautiful simple game, yet wildly complicated. A lot of chips can be lost whilst holding four of a kind or even a straight flush. On the other side of the scale a hand can be won by a simple Jack high. The song 'THE GAMBLER,' contains the lyrics, "Know when to hold'em … know when to fold'em." A player should strive to minimise his losses when he has an inferior hand by recognising the value of his holding cards in comparison to those of his opponents. As for safe-guarding chips, the worst hand can turn out to be the second best hand on the table. A fine example of this is that a full hand is highly unlikely to fold against four of a kind whereas a no pair hand is likely to fold very quickly.

This is a story about ten experienced hungry players and the humorous, tragic and poignant events that happen in the life of a poker player. There are millions of poker players throughout the world who thoroughly enjoy the magical game. On saying that they are all fully aware that every player loves to bluff. To win a hand under normal conditions is great but, to win it with a bluff is phenomenal! Now this story is related to ten players gathered around a poker table geared up for a contest of 'Texas Hold'em Poker'. The outcome of the game unfolds as it actually happens but, as it comes around to each player's call, there is a flashback into parts of his life. What is written within the pages is what has been related to me. But the question is ... is it true or is it fiction? I'll let you be the judge of that. They are all poker players and it's nigh impossible to know whether they are telling the truth or whether it is just a myth.

Consequently, my book is neither non fiction nor fiction ... it can only be described as FACTION.

DEDICATION

D edicated to Sunny, a gentleman who loved the game of poker. He was a very friendly man and an inspiration to everyone who knew him.

He is sadly missed.

CHAPTER 1 - LEARNING THE GAME

Poker is a game well loved by millions of people around the globe. I am an eighty-two year old man and, as far as playing poker is concerned, I can only be described as a raw beginner. And yet I found myself sat at a poker table along with nine very experienced canny players and we were about to embark on a very special game. As I gazed around the table at the nine men, all from totally different backgrounds, I began to wonder how on earth I found myself in this position. Up until the previous three years I had never ever indulged in any type of poker. I didn't even understand the rudiments of the game.

And so I asked myself, "How come I am sat amongst these elite players ... why me?"

It was then that my mind began to drift back to how it came about.

I was born on April 11th 1939 and I have had a varied and interesting life. As a child, together with Mum and Dad, two brothers and three sisters, we lived together in a two-up, two-down terraced house that was full of rising damp. A broken flag floor in the living room didn't conserve any heat from a fire set in and old cast iron fireplace. There was no lighting in the house except for an old antiquated gas lamp that hung low from the ceiling with a gas mantle. There were no washing facilities within the house except for a cold water tap over a pot sink. To go to the loo we had to negotiate fourteen steep stone steps to where a long drop lavatory was housed in an old air raid shelter. To venture out on a cold wintry night was like sending a lemming out to meet its doom. But despite living in these dank conditions, for the first twenty years of my life, I was always a happy child.

I was born on 11th April 1939 just months prior to the outbreak of the Second World War. It was ironic as the First World War ended at eleven o'clock and this one started at eleven o'clock on 3rd September. Curfews were implemented and orders issued to put up window blinds so as not to show even a chink of light. As a child I clearly recall days of the blackout and the sounds of sirens warning of an air raid attack. During these times people went into air raid shelters which had been built in their back yards. My mum refused to do this and, when she heard the sound of German planes droning overhead, she would always tuck us up in bed and say a little prayer, "Lord if my children are going to die then let it be in the comfort of their beds rather than in a dark dank air raid shelter where they could be buried alive and suffer a horrible death."

To help boost morale during the dark days many jokes were written weekly about the blackout in the Burnley Express.

A woman had just bought some fish 'n' chips and she had a strong aroma about her.

As she was trying to find her way home by groping her hands along the walls of houses, a man knocked her down.

On picking her up he apologised, "I'm awfully sorry luv ... I thought tha' wer't door to chippy!"

During the war years German U-boats sank many British ships in the Atlantic and prevented shipments of food reaching England's shores and consequently, this lead to food rationing. In a way it was good because it prevented rich people from over buying. Rationing and price controls and the fact that many individuals began to grow food in allotments meant that people were eating better than ever before. It appeared that the wartime diet was very healthy, albeit somewhat limited.

I well remember the end of the war as droves of excited people were singing and dancing as they passed by our house making their way to the Town Hall on Manchester Road. On following them I was fascinated to see gas lamps and the Town Hall clock lit up for the first time in my life. I was amazed to see thousands of people dancing the conga and singing Auld Lang Syne and lots of war songs. Bands magically appeared from nowhere, men were clanging dustbin lids together whilst women played kitchen utensils and rang bells. I was only six years old but I knew I was witnessing an expression of public joy that I would never ever see again in my lifetime. I was completely mesmerised by the hullabaloo around me ... it was like being in Wonderland.

However, even though the war was over, food rationing continued right up until 1954.

****

My dad was a rag-and-bone man and had been to prison twice. Consequently, during my junior school days, I, along with my brothers and sisters, had to put up with many barbed comments in the schoolyard. This was the cause of many fights we had to endure through our formative years. One particular incident I well remember. It was playtime and I had just left the classroom when Peter Birtwhistle and Paul Whitham approached me.

"Hiya Cowheel ... canya dad fly?"

"What are you talking about Birtwhistle?" I responded.

"Well he's a bird in't he? A jailbird ... ha ha!"

"Yeah, and I bet he's with all the murderers," mocked Paul Whitham.

"Get lost!" I retaliated. "He's a better dad than yours anyroad."

"Oh aye ... you mean when he's not in jail."

"Don't stand for that our John," shouted my brother Jimmy, who'd just heard the stinging comments from across the yard, "get him thumped!"

"Lay off it our kid," I replied, trying to play down the situation, "I'll handle it my way."

"Handle it your way," sneered Birtwhistle. What you mean is you're frightened to death!"

"Don't start something you can't finish Birtwhistle!" growled our Jimmy.

"Why, what will you do Cowheel ... put me in a padded cell with your dad?"

"A padded cell ... what the flamin' 'eck are you talking about?"

By now a crowd of lads had gathered and to their amusement, Birtwhistle burst out laughing and came out with another crushing insult.

"Well, he'll be in a padded cell won't he, padded out wi' a load o' rags off the rag cart ... ha ha ha!"

Enough said, our Jimmy's composure changed from controlled to seething anger. "You swine!" he shrieked, his face red with rage. Within seconds both lads were exchanging blows knocking hell out of each other. All the kids formed a circle and the sound of, "A fight ... a fight," resounded around the schoolyard.

I felt the tension building up inside me as the air vibrated. Consequently, I too ended up rolling about on the concrete floor fighting with Whitham. I'd lost a few fights in this yard but this was different. I'd been goaded into the fight and my adrenaline was flowing.

"Right Whitham," I thought "it's either you or me. I laid into him for all I was worth and didn't let up until we were both exhausted and suffering from a few bruises. I was quite happy with the outcome and more so because Whitham never bothered me again after that.

My siblings and I were to have more fights in that yard over the years but we gradually gained the respect of our peers and lots of us became friends for life.

I wrote the following poem about it:

JUNIOR SCHOOL

St Thomas's was the name of our school,

All the kids were poor but ever so cool.

Wearing steel bottomed clogs that made a great sound,

We created bright sparks by kicking the ground.

At nine on the dot into single file we fell,

Then marched into class to the sound of a bell.

Paraded like soldiers dressed in our togs,

Clip clop clip clop ... went the sound of our clogs.

At playtime we used to play in a yard,

I soon learnt I had to be hard.

The yard was concrete and ... much to my plight

In that very yard ... I had my first fight.

Sparks from clogs ... shouts and jeers,

Left many a black eye filled with tears.

T'was a hard life ... but not quite so cruel,

No biting, no kicking ... we all stuck to the rule.

Life is quite strange and through all that strife,

Lots of us kids became friends for life.

I never had any money in my pocket but, armed with a few fag packets, I was always assured of some tuck. Playing fag cards, where two lads knelt down on the kerb and flicked fag packets at a target card stood up against a wall was the 'in game'. The lad who knocked down the target card readily scooped up the lot. I was a good player and never went short of tuck. One of my mates, Desmond Lee, always came to school with sixpence, which was enough to buy a packet of dates from the tuck shop. I loved this exotic fruit and would gladly exchange ten faggies for a handful. I felt confident I could easily replace my losses. A lad could have his arse end hanging out but, if he had a few fag packets in his pocket, he was happy. I always had plenty of 'faggies' because, besides being a good player, I used to regularly raid the paper mill where there were bails stacked full of mint rare fag packets. To get into the mill I had to nimbly balance on top of a long steel pipe which spanned over a swift running river. I routinely retrieved a sack full of cards and therefore, even if I didn't win many games at school, I still had my secret stack to fall back on. Woodbine, Captain and Park Drive fag packets were plentiful but Passing Cloud and Miss Blanche were rare and therefore more exchangeable. But the most prestigious and sought after card was, as the name implies, 'Royalty'. It was the 'king' of cards. One day whilst raiding the mill I came across a bail stacked with the desirable cards and they were all in pristine condition. I couldn't believe my luck ... I felt like a millionaire. In the schoolyard I was the envy of my mates ... I never went short of tuck for months after that.

Mum could never give us any money but I always had a few pennies in my pocket due to some enterprising schemes. Our house was close to a main railway line and winters were cold in those damp terraced houses. I regularly used to pick coal from the railway lines and sell it to the neighbours and also to keep the fire burning in our house. Also I had a make-do trolley that I'd made from old pram wheels and I would pick up bags of cinders for the neighbours from a gas depot on Parker Lane. I charged sixpence a trip so I was well happy. Another scheme was to take empty beer bottles back to the Labour Club at one penny a bottle. I would scale a high wall at the back entrance, steal a few bottles from stacked crates, and then smarmily return them through the front door. Another venture which I thoroughly enjoyed was taking neighbours' heirlooms to the pawn shop on Lord Street and redeeming them later on pay day. I became well known amongst the neighbours and the pawn broker alike and I always got them the going rate. I only charged pennies for the service but I was happy at that and quite content with my lot.

****

Life carried on much the same in this vein and on leaving school at the age of fifteen I went working down a coal mine. I spent nine years in total working underground interrupted by two years National Service in the Royal Army Medical Corps.

The fifties were great years, especially for teenagers ... I relished every moment. However, at the age of seventeen, I had a bad experience concerning our local milkman. It was quite traumatic for me and dampened my ego somewhat making me feel humiliated and ashamed. His name was Harold White.

He delivered milk to many households on Albion Street and his mode of transport was a horse and cart. He would often tether his horse to the gas lamp outside our house and, many a time, I would feed it a carrot.

Harry was in his early thirties and renowned for his fine physique and his reputation of having served in the Royal Marines, a commando outfit. Many a person would comment that he was as strong as an ox.

The incident happened one Saturday night after thoroughly enjoying myself dancing in the Empress Ballroom to the sound of Ted Heath and his band. All my mates had clicked, leaving me a little despondent as I made my way home.

"Not to worry," I thought, "better luck next week. Anyroad, I'm starving ... I'll just tek' myself off to the chippy for some nosh."

The Chippy was next door to the 'Coach and Horses' Pub about two 200 yards from the dancehall. As I stood in the queue waiting for my fish 'n' chips I noticed Harry in front of me.

"All reight young fella," he smiled cheerfully, "you're a Trafalgar Waller aren't you?"

"Yeah I am," I responded, "I live on Albion Street ... mi mam's one o' your customers."

"I thought I knew your face, you're the lad who feeds my horse wi' a carrot now and then. Anyroad, you look as if you've enjoyed yourself ... have you been dancing?"

"Yeah I have," I gloated, "I've been down th'Empess Ballroom with some o' mi' mates ... it's an absolutely fantastic place."

"Your mates," he queried, "how come they're not here with you?"

"'Cos the lucky sods have all got fixed up ... I'm the only one who's missed out. Not to worry though, that's how the cookie crumbles ... I'll just have to settle for fish 'n' chips."

Tha' could do a lot worse lad," he grinned, "at least it'll keep thi' out o' trouble eh?"

"Aye you could be right there," I mumbled as I stuffed a chip into my mouth, "but chance would o' been a fine thing. Anyroad, I'll be seeing you ... so long!"

"Hang on a minute young fella, it's a long way to Albion Street," he said as I attempted to pass him, "I'll give thi' a lift in mi' car if tha' wants ... I'm only parked on t'other side o' road."

"Aye alright, fair enough Harry," I replied not thinking anything about it, "that'll be great." I felt comfortable with the situation until we'd crossed over to the other side of the road and I couldn't see any signs of a car. He started to walk towards a large expanse of derelict ground at the back of the Odeon Cinema where large steel factory boilers were stored. As a child I'd played amongst these gigantic boilers and knew only too well that the canal ran just shortly beyond them. The spare land had no lighting and the Odeon cast a dark shadow over the area making it pitch black and eerie.

As he walked into the eerie darkness I got strong vibes telling me that something was afoot. My instinct told me that he was up to no good and common sense took over. "There's no way I'm going behind them boilers with him," I thought, "I don't even think he's got a car. He more likely wants to try it on with me ... no chance!"

"Are you comin' then?" he shouted from the shadows interrupting my thoughts, "my car's over yonder near the canal"

"U-umph, no way," I mumbled, "on your bike!"

"What's that? he shouted.

"Oh now't Harry," I lied through my teeth, "on second thoughts, I've decided to leg it home ... it's a lovely night and I feel like some fresh air."

Without further ado, I took my leave and walked sprightly past the dancehall towards St James' Street.

"The dirty ole' git," I kept saying to myself as I strolled through the town centre, "why doesn't he find himself a woman?"

Then, just as I was turning the corner at the bottom of Manchester Road, Harry pulled up alongside me in his car. "Well," he said, leaning out of the passenger window, "do you still want a lift or what ... the offer's still on?"

I was rather taken aback ... he really did have a car. I felt shamefaced for mistrusting him and my suspicions vanished. With my confidence restored I accepted the lift and got into the passenger seat. I felt relaxed as he laughed and joked whilst driving up Manchester Road; but I became uneasy when he speeded up and drove past Trafalgar Street.

"Whoa Harry!" I shouted, "You've passed Trafalgar ... can you drop me off at Piccadilly Road?"

He paid no heed to me and put his foot down on the gas and sped for the outskirts of town.

"Whoa, whaddaya think you're doin'? I spluttered in panic. "Let me out ... you're goin' miles out o' my way!"

"Eh don't worry about it lad," he grinned smarmily as he put his hand onto the inside of my leg caressing my thigh. "If it's a good time tha's after, I'm gonna tek' thi' to a nightclub in Rawtenstall where we can have a ball."

I was now frightened as my initial suspicions flooded back to me. The very thought of being driven by this man into the open countryside absolutely terrified me. But, despite the terror that ran through my being, I kept my wits about me … I knew I had to come up with something quick. We were fast reaching the summit traffic lights and I prayed they would be on red so that I could make a quick getaway. I was aware that the bleak expanse of "Crown Point' lay beyond the lights and I had visions of this monster having his wicked way with me. My fear intensified as my imagination saw me lying dead in a ditch on the open moors. To my utter dismay, the lights were on green and he sped through them at breakneck speed.

"Come on John, think o' something afore it's too late," I prayed. I was young, fit and strong, but I knew I was no match for this powerful man. By God's intervention it came to me that I had to play this guy at his own game. Luckily for me, there was a tiny slip road, which turned back on itself just prior to Bull and Butcher Pub.

"Harry," I said nudging him and giving him the eye, I know a great place in Padiham where we can have a fantastic time. Just turn down this snicket back onto Rossendale Avenue and I'll take you there." To my relief he took me at my word.

"Great," he said turning the corner on two wheels, "now you're talking!"

"Thank goodness for that," I sighed with relief, "at least it's given me some leeway."

I had to keep calm but inwardly prayed that traffic lights at Rosegrove Junction would be on red. No such luck ... they were on green and he sped through them like Stirling Moss. I began to panic again as my chances of escaping, before we reached Padiham where my bluff would be called, were fast running out.

As he accelerated towards the final main junction I geared myself up mentally to risk life and limb by jumping out of the car rather than let this evil pervert get his filthy paws on me. I was still a virgin and terrified of being sexually abused by this depraved monster; the very thought made my skin crawl. Once again I pictured myself being found dead somewhere in open countryside. The thought of my grief stricken mother and family stirred me on. I placed my hand on the car's door handle and prepared myself for the worst. But then, God smiled down on me. A large wagon speeding down Padiham road forced Harry to slow down.

I didn't need a second chance ... in a flash I leapt out of the car and ran like a bat out of hell ... Roger Bannister couldn't have caught me. I made my way to the nearest field and bolted over a stone wall and crouched in a corner like a frightened rabbit. I shook uncontrollably and for the life in me I daren't move. I was rooted to the spot, cold and bedraggled and I remained there until dawn. I didn't dare lift my head for fear of seeing his beady eyes bearing down on me. Gradually though I regained enough courage to scan the area in every direction, but my adrenaline was flowing and I was ready to make a bolt for it at any sign of danger. As I made my way homewards I was still on tenterhooks and constantly glanced over my shoulder.

Although I came out of the ordeal unscathed bodily it affected me inasmuch as I felt ashamed. It may seem silly but, for many years to come, I never mentioned it to a living soul. If I had mentioned it to my mam she would certainly have gone to the police station. I didn't want this because I was frightened that I would get ridiculed at work by my workmates ... especially in the showers. I gave it a lot of thought and, rightly or wrongly, I decided it was one secret that I would keep to myself.

Consequently my confidence suffered somewhat. I was an innocent victim and maybe I shouldn't have felt that way, but I did. Like a lot of victims of atrocity I felt as though I was somehow to blame ... had I encouraged him in any way by giving out wrong signals? But then common sense prevailed ... clearly I hadn't, I was just a normal teenager enjoying a good night out. In my anguish my heart went out to people who'd been the victims of sexual assault and how terribly helpless and alone they must have felt.

"There but for the grace of God go I," I thought.

The secret was to remain within me until I was in my sixties. It was only when I began to write my memoirs that I decided to bring my ordeal into the open and lay my ghost to rest. Yes, I'd kept the secret to myself for fear of ridicule from my mining colleagues and friends. The stigma of guilt, shame and humiliation stayed with me throughout my life. Even in adulthood I often shuddered of what might have happened.

I never set eyes on Harry again ... he'd most likely absconded thinking I would report him to the police.

Looking back in hindsight I should have exposed him, but I was too ashamed and lacking in confidence.

Ironically, shortly after my ordeal, I saw some graffiti on the wall of a public toilet. which read:

HARRY WHITE THE BUMBOY.

"U-um, "I thought, "he's obviously been trying it on elsewhere ...I'm not the only one who knows about him."

****

Working alongside hardworking men in the bowels of the earth, the boy very soon became the man. Sweat dripped from the brows of hard working men as they courageously battled relentlessly against the elements. Labouring constantly in the depth of the earth in a dark, damp and dusty environment, the life of each man dependent on the other, these men really were the salt of the earth. There was a comradeship second to none and there was never any backbiting. If a disagreement took place between two men it would be argued out during bait time and that was the end of it. The two men involved would then get down to the gritty task and work arduously alongside their team mates. I thoroughly enjoyed this aspect of·mine working. The work was hard and dangerous but I admired watching laborious men striving to strip the coal seam to keep the home fires burning. On reaching the age of twenty I was called upon to serve two years National Service and placed into the Royal

Army Medical Corps. I enjoyed sports but I was never a good footballer or cricketer. But I was very fit and excelled at table tennis and swimming. Most of my army time was spent in Cameroon, West Africa. Up to the age of twenty, prior to going to Africa, I had lived in Burnley, a Lancashire cotton town, in a small dank terraced house on a very steep stone cobbled street. It was set in an area of town known as the 'Weaver's Triangle.' It was so called because lots of weaving sheds were built close together alongside the Leeds and Liverpool Canal and large factory chimneys belched out thick contaminated smoke which hung over the town houses like a shroud. In Burnley there were more tall factory chimneys than any other town in the world. Hence, going to a sunny climate beckoned me.

I was brought up in abject poverty or so I thought. It was only when I reached Africa that I began to realise what true impoverishment meant. The poor inhabitants strived daily to earn a few coppers in order to make ends meet. Most of them lived within thick jungle territory in little mud huts with a straw roof and there were no commodities like water, gas or electricity at their disposal. I used to be enthralled as I watched young girls carrying large vases of water on their heads which they had carried from a far off river. I worked alongside these poor souls in field hospitals in outlying jungle territory and found them to be humble and reliable. Despite their poor living conditions I found these poor indigenous people very friendly and generous to a fault ... they had nothing but would gladly give you the shirt of their back. I was so taken aback by their plight that I got involved more than I should have done. If anyone of them became ill I would take medical supplies to their little mud huts in the middle of nowhere and help them with as best I could. Just like the soldiers on camp, young native boys and girls often suffered deep lacerations to their hands and arms simply by walking through elephant grass. The wounds were often quite wide and needed several stitches followed by a dose of antibiotics. There was no medical assistance at hand for these poor souls and so, what was I supposed to do. If I didn't help them the wound would definitely become infected. I was aware that if, what I was doing, got back to my commanding officer I would be thrown into the brig with loss of pay. Nevertheless, it was a risk I was willing to take ... I'd recently spent a week in the jail and I was prepared to do it again. At times a parent would approach me if a small child was suffering from a fever with a rip roaring temperature. The best I could do was to supply them with medicine and lots of orange cordial to encourage the infant to drink a lot. Also I taught them how to sponge the youngster down so as to lower their temperature. I only did little things for them but they were eternally grateful and thought I was a king. Every time I went to the local market place I was surrounded by many locals and I became known as Dr John.

One particular incident readily springs to my mind. I was off duty and decided to hire a rowing boat. As I rowed down a slow flowing river I passed many small fishing boats with nets cast over the sides. The river was about thirty five yards wide and as I passed many mangrove bushes it put me in mind of when I'd spent hours in a swamp whilst out on patrol in the jungle with a troop of infantry men. About three miles downstream I anchored onto an embankment where some fishermen were just bringing in their catch and was immediately greeted by locals with big beams on their faces.

"Welcome Johnny!" said a stockily-built fellow, who appeared to be the tribe leader, "you are much welcome to our humble home." I wondered how he knew my name but then I realised that they called all English men Johnny.

As I was paraded into the hamlet many natives were sat around a camp fire which young girls were energetically stoking with wood, which they had just carried on their heads from a surrounding jungle. Suspended over the fire was a gigantic wok on a grid, held up by chains hanging from a steel bar. Some women prepared the fish on a spit whilst others cooked chopped up potatoes and strange looking vegetables in the huge wok. The fish was then cut up into small segments and placed into the wok to make one big stew. Elderly adults and typical pot bellied children looked on in earnest, their nostrils sniffing the air as the aroma drifted towards them. Their eyes were riveted on the large cooking utensil as the heap of chopped up food sizzled away. The children's eagerness to savour the meal was obvious as they smacked their lips, wetting them with saliva. This was to be their first modest meal in days and yet, hungry as they were, they waited patiently for the dinner ladies to serve out their portions. The ladies scooped up small portions from the wok using a ladle and served them on small tin plates.

The wok was then taken from above the fire and allowed to cool for a while on the ground. Men then squatted around the now large communal pan on their haunches and ate from it by breaking bread and dipping it into the stew with their bare hands using just their fingers.

With a gesture born of natural habit, one of the ladies turned and invited me to eat. Once again I was taken aback by their humility and kindness. I was a stranger to them and yet they were willing to share what bit of food they had.

I didn't eat much but I found it to be a very pleasant experience as one man offered me some kind of wine in a tin canister. It was after our little feast that I noticed some young girls carrying water using a bough broken from a tree and carved to fit their shoulders. The yoke was cautiously pivoted around their necks and a small pot suspended by string dangled from each end. As I watched it took me back to my childhood as it reminded of an amusing fable that my mother told me. I'd always liked the tale and decided to tell it to the youngsters.

As they sat down in a group all willing and eager to listen I related it to them:

"There was a little girl who lived in a small village much like this one and she had to fetch water from a river which was a long way off. Just like you she carried two small pots on the end of a yoke. Now the little girl was very fond of her two little pots and used to polish and talk to them every day. She was a happy child and her two little pots were very happy as well. All was well with the world, but sadly, one day one of the pots got damaged and developed a long crack in it. Now every time she went to collect water the girl would fill the two pots to the brim, but on returning to the village the damaged urn was almost empty. The young girl didn't mind, but the little pot did; it became a very unhappy little pot.

'What's to do my little friend?' she asked one day, 'You seem so unhappy.'

'I am unhappy,' replied the little pot with tears running down the length of the crack, 'I'm useless, simply useless; I can't carry water any more.'

'But you're not useless,' stressed the little girl stroking its rim. 'In fact you're more useful now than you've ever been.'

'You're only saying that to make me feel better,' whimpered the little vessel, 'I'm absolutely useless; I'm nothing but a little crackpot!"'

Much to my surprise that remark sparked off a fit of laughter amongst the native children. I was surprised because I didn't think they would get the little joke as it was intended. But they certainly did and it created a happy atmosphere. That was good but the moral of the story had a far deeper meaning ... albeit pleasant.

"Right children," I said, "I'm glad you liked that, but let's find out what happened next shall we."

"Oh yes please!" they all chanted in unison, expressing their approval.

I then continued with the little parable:

"'You're no such thing,' said the little girl reassuringly, 'you are a very important water carrier and I can prove it to you.'

'Oh yeah, and how can you do that?' sniffed the poor little crock.

Untying the tiny jug from the yoke she cradled it in her hands and carried it to the edge of the village.

'There,' she said, looking back along a trodden path that stretched way down to the river, 'do you see anything?'

The poor thing looked as hard as it could but, try as it may, it wasn't too sure exactly what she wanted it to look for.

'What do you mean,' it asked, 'what is it you want me to see?'

'Ah,' she answered, 'just look to the right hand side of the path and you will see that the land is barren.'

'That's right,' said the little jug now quite bemused.

'You see,' said the little girl, 'that is the side on which I carried the other pot which was full of water. Now my friend, look to the left hand side of the path ... what do you see there?'

To the tiny vessel's surprise the land on the other side of the trodden path was laden with flowers all the way back to the river.

'I don't understand,' it said, 'what's happened?"

'Well my precious pot," she said lovingly, "that is the side on which I carried you and every day you have been leaking and watering the soil all the way from the river to the village. Because of you all these beautiful flowers have *grown and prospered: without you they would have withered and died. You have actually turned barren land into a fertile oasis. I know all the other pots have done a good job, but so have you my precious little friend. Now do you see how useful you have been?'*

The little pot smiled and had to acknowledge what it had done. From that day on it was carried by the little girl and continued to water the flowers and was forever after a very happy little jug."

After the tale the children showed their appreciation by clapping loudly and displaying big wide smiles on their faces. They seemed to have enjoyed it. I know that I did when I heard it as a boy and it had stayed within me ever since.

By now it was time to head back to camp. The natives saw me to my boat and cheerfully waved me off as I headed back upstream. It had been a wonderful day and I couldn't wait to tell my mates of my little enterprise. It was certainly one I will never forget.

****

On leaving the army I spent another four years working down Deerplay Coalmine situated on Bacup moor. The mine closed down and so I undertook a government joinery course.

I felt confident and got a job for 'Lancashire Shop Fitters' in Oswaldtwistle. It was a great firm and my task, along with a mate, was to refit shops all over England, Scotland and Wales. I was actually working in Clydebank, Glasgow when my son, Craig, was born. The following week I was working in a shop in Land's End, Cornwall. Another time I worked in Portree on the Isle of Skye. During the course of six years I travelled the length and breadth of England Scotland and Wales. It certainly taught me the geography of the British Isles. A sad time I clearly remember happened at 9-05am on 21st of October 1966 in a tiny village in south Wales. I was working close by in Merthyr Tydfil when a coal mining disaster, that shocked the nation, occurred in Aberfan, a small village. An avalanche of slack coal cascaded down a mountainside and buried a school, taking the lives of 116 children and 28 adults. A tip, which had been created on a mountain slope above Aberfan, overlaid a natural spring. A period of heavy rain led to a build up of slurry and this caused a catastrophic collapse of the tip. Sadly, thousands of tons of slurry and shale gushed down the mountain completely engulfing the school and 28 houses. The sad ironic thing is that the children had only been in their classrooms five minutes when it happened.

****

I worked at that firm for five years and then decided to set up my own joinery business. I took on grant work from the Council and full house refurbishments. I did all the joinery and ground work myself but I sub-contracted out to electricians, bricklayers, plumbers etc... By the age of 38 I had prospered and built up a nice portfolio of houses and also paid for my own home. By now I was married and had two sons. I felt quite secure and decided on another career. I'd thoroughly enjoyed my army life working in field hospitals ... it came so natural to me and so I applied to train in the medical profession.

After three years training I qualified as a State Registered Nurse and commenced working on the Accident and Emergency Dept at Burnley General Hospital. My army training put me in good stead and helped me to cope with horrific road traffic accidents and other bad mishaps.

It was about this time that I went on holiday to Tenerife and I noticed that people from many different countries could all speak English. It got me to thinking that we English are lazy and I made up my mind to start learning Spanish from that day forward.

I enjoyed working on the Casualty Department, but at the age of 58, due to my partner Ann, being seriously ill, I took early retirement. She was suffering from renal failure and had to attend Accrington Victoria Hospital three times a week for dialysis.

During my retirement I reflected back onto my childhood days. I then fulfilled a promise to my mother and decided to write her biography on how she brought six of us up during the Second World War. The book took off more than I expected and I received letters from all over the world. But shortly after the book was published Ann died. It was a very low point in my life ... I was devastated and decided to change my way of life. I'd been attending Preston University studying for my degree in Spanish, but I couldn't face studying anymore. Since then I have travelled to many parts of the globe. Greece, France, Germany, Dominican Republic and Bali are just a few, but the main country I visited was Spain. I was so intrigued by their culture that I delved into it more. Throughout Spain nearly every area has its own special legend and one of particular interest is 'El Camino de Santiago de Compostela.' It is a well known pilgrimage in Northern Spain that has been ongoing since the 9th century. Translated to 'The Path of Saint James,' it is a route that starts in a small French village called 'St Jean Pea de Paul' and finishes in Santiago, a distance of over five hundred miles. The first day's trek is a fourteen mile uphill climb over the Pyrenees Mountains and a five mile descent into Spain. The journey continues through rocky mountainous terrain passing through many tiny Spanish hamlets where the locals cannot speak a word of English. Over two million pilgrims make the arduous journey every year footslogging it with heavy back packs on their backs. Along the way there are many 'albergues' (hostels) where pilgrims can spend the night. The hostels are run by volunteers and the cost is minimal and sometimes optional. At times there can be up to eighty people in an albergue, men and women alike, but everyone is discreet and things work out fine. People from all walks of life congregate together and the feeling of friendliness is incredible. Every village supplies a 'pilgrim's menu of the day', which includes a three course meal and a bottle of wine. All the pilgrims get together and celebrate after a hard day's slog with a sing along and the atmosphere created is indescribable.

During my retirement I, along with my friend, Fred Uttley, made the pain staking journey eight times in order to raise money for impoverished countries throughout the world. On our first attempt we raised over four thousand pounds to help the poor impoverished 'Street Children of Brazil,' who were living in sewers. Young children, only eight years old, were striving to survive and take care of younger ones. The 'Powers That Be' treats them as vermin and police guards randomly round them up and shoot the poor little mites. Surely, something has to be done to stop this terrible atrocity.

After our first pilgrimage all our efforts were to raise money for whatever worthy cause there was in the world whether it be war torn countries, natural disasters or impoverished countries like Africa.

Being able to speak the language Fred and I became quite experienced and well known on the Camino and CAFOD, a well known Catholic charity, asked us act as guides for fourteen would-be pilgrims. It wasn't an easy task as some were elderly and slow walkers. Hence, sometimes the albergues were full and we had to sleep outdoors under the stars. But it turned out well and the event raised more than fourteen thousand pounds and the money was used to build a small school and a water well in an African village. This took my mind back many years to when I was serving my National Service in Kumba, Cameroon, amongst the poor inhabitants.

As years passed, I still kept up my walking, but it was not quite so mountainous this time. In fact, it was very flat. Along with my little dog I walked the length of the Leeds & Liverpool Canal from Barrowford Locks to Liverpool and back. It took me about fifteen days and I passed by fifty locks altogether and each one was ten feet deep. Throughout the journey, each lock was downhill and so I calculated that Liverpool is exactly 500 feet lower than Barrowford. Hence, the lowest point of Burnley is approximately the same height as the top of Blackpool Tower.

At the age of 74 I went to America and whilst I was in Colorado I visited a national Park called Mesa Verde which translates to A Green Table. It is a renowned canyon where Red Indians used to live in cliff dwellings. To reach the dwellings I had to scale high wooden ladders attached to sheer cliff walls. After that I travelled to Arizona and decided to raft down the Colorado River, deep within the Grand Canyon. I covered 187 miles negotiating many white water rapids and spent about ten nights on a sandy shore gazing up at the heavens from way down in the abyss. As sheer stone cliffs towered above me the stars appeared to be magnified against a dark background. It was an experience that I cannot put into words ... one has to do it to experience it for themselves.

Then at the age of 76 I decided to go to Perth, Australia and that is where I met Elsina, a South American lady. She was born in Suriname, close to where the film 'Papilon,' starring Steve McQueen, was made. I knew from the moment I set eyes on her that she was the girl for me. We courted for over two years and then she became my wife and fulfilled an empty void in my life. From Perth we both travelled to Tasmania and explored many mountainous regions. We settled for a while in an alpine village called Scottsdale and it was here in a club that I encountered a poker competition known as 'Texas Hold'em.'

Now in all my worldly experience I had never played the game of poker. I had played many card games in the past but I had never indulged in poker. As I watched I became quite intrigued observing the expressions on the players' faces as each one either checked, called, raised or folded their cards. On enquiring I was told it was a knockout tournament and it was called Texas Hold'em. The more I watched them play the more intrigued I became and by the end of the night I had booked an appointment for the next session. I learnt that the sessions were held every Wednesday and Friday evenings and for the rest of my time in Tasmania I never missed a session. It didn't take me long to realise that poker is a great leveller. By that I mean that it brings people together from all walks of life. For example I looked around the poker table and the first person was Darrel, a retired policeman. He was the same age as me and was a very experienced sharp player.

Then there was Ray, a brick layer's labourer who was always short of cash.

Sat by him was Jason, a rather wealthy land owner who always played alongside his mate Jay Jay.

Sitting opposite me was Dawn, a nurse. She was quite a lady but she certainly knew how to play this game. Sitting next to Dawn was her friend Kylie, a housewife. At first I thought it would be easy playing against these ladies but I soon changed my mind ... they were both as good as it comes.

Then came Robert, another extremely wealthy man. He owned a very large farm and used to supply all the supermarkets and other places with vegetables.

Finally sat on my right was Glen, an electrician. Glen was a gentleman and I clicked with him from the word go. He and his wife had a smallholding where he kept pigs, chickens and a few cows. He regularly invited me round and I thoroughly enjoyed watching him feed some newly born calves.

All these people were from different backgrounds but there was a common denominator ... they all loved and took poker very seriously. Whether it was Ray or Jason, they strived to win each hand. I soon discovered that none of them liked to lose. On saying that, when they did lose they took it in good spirits. Usually there were about 27 players which meant that three tables were in play. Looking about the room, everybody chatted away like one big happy family.

"Yes," I thought to myself, "this game truly brings people together from all walks of life."

The starting stack was always 9000 chips and the blinds were 25/50. Due to my inexperience of the game I was constantly knocked out early into each session but it didn't dampen my enthusiasm. In fact the more I lost the more determined I became to get the gist of the game. Then after about 10 games things started to brighten up. In the next five games I finished 5th, 4th, 3rd, 2nd respectively and then finally ... I won! Well now my enthusiasm for the game had taken over and I became addicted to the game ... I had won it once and I felt sure I could do it again. I went into my next bout full of confidence thinking that I had mastered the game. I couldn't have been more wrong ... the next four sessions I went crashing out in the early rounds just like I was a raw beginner. And to be truthful, that's exactly what I was. I knew I was doing something wrong and so I turned to my computer for advice. Consequently I came across a statement which quoted that poker is an easy game to learn but impossible to master.

"No ... this can't be," I thought, "I've only been playing a few weeks and I've already won one tournament and I feel sure I'm going to win a lot more."

Well, in the following weeks I did win another tournament and, once again, my confidence was sky high.

However, yet again, my new found confidence soon came crashing down as I then began to lose one game after another. Many a time, certain I would win, I'd go all in with two large pairs only to be beaten by a straight or a flush. I well remember the first time I went 'All In' with a nut flush only to be beaten by a full house. Mind you, during my learning process I didn't really study the show cards like I should have. For example if there was a pair showing on the board I didn't spot the danger of a set, a full house, or even four of a kind. Also I didn't have a clue on positional play and how important it is to take note of how your opponents are betting.

Another fault I had was that I didn't realise the importance of a good kicker. If I had an ace in my hand I was keen to bet on it. One painful lesson I had was when I picked up an Ace/8 unsuited. The blinds were 1000/2000 and I had a stack of 22000 in front of me. It happened to be my deal and before the flop Darrel bet 2000. Both Ray and Jason called and I called as well. Already there was 11000 in the pot and the flop was 2/7/Ace. Darrel raised it to 5000 and Jason called. Ray folded and I called ... the pot was now 26000. I was a little wary but then came the turn card which happened to be another Ace. "Wow!" I thought, "All those lovely chips in the pot are mine."

To my surprise and delight, Darrel raised it a further 5000. This time Jason folded but I willingly called. The river card was a nine and Darrel checked. I weighed up the show cards and it was impossible for Darrel to have a straight or a flush.

"U-Um" I mumbled to myself after studying hard, "I've got a set of Aces here ... the only way he can beat me is with pocket 2's, 7's or 9's for a full house". After my deliberation I shoved in my remaining chips and called 'All In'. To my surprise he called me.

"I've got three aces Darrel," I said rather smugly.

"So have I," he replied with a smile on his face ... and he followed that with a J.

"Oh no!" I grunted, realising that I had never taken my kicker card into account. I'd no option but to put it down to experience and I've been wary of kickers ever since.

Another time that I took a good beating was when I had pocket Aces. However on this occasion I didn't do anything wrong; it was just one of those things that happen in this magical game. Once again I was in prime position as the dealer. The first four players folded and Peter, a young teenager went All In with 56000 chips. All the other players folded and it just left me heads up against the youngster ... and I had a stack of 60000 chips.

"Well," I thought, "if I don't call in this situation I might as well not play poker." So consequently I called and on the turn of cards the young lad had A/8. I was quite happy with that but the flop was Q/K/8 giving him a slight chance. The turn card was a 6 but then, to my dismay ... the river card was another eight. Instead of doubling my stack of chips I was now down to 4000.

I was disappointed with that result but, once again, I had no choice but to put it down to experience. As time went on I found the game to be uncanny and that it swung in roundabouts, like the time I got pocket eights. Six players bet before the flop and I called. The flop was A/K/8 and four players called a 4000 bet and I did the same. To my sheer delight the turn card was another eight. I had four eights and Darrel- was the first player and he went All In, with 6000 chips and to my surprise Ray and Donna called. I was the last player and they all looked at me expecting me to fold.

"Righto," I said looking a bit down in the mouth, "I'll call!"

Darrell was the first to show his cards and even before the river card he had a full house with pocket Kings and both Ray and Donna had two large pairs. It didn't matter what the river card was to be ... I just couldn't be beat as Donna had the other King. It was a fantastic feeling and I got a rush of adrenaline as I scooped up a massive stack of chips. I was now by far the chip leader and felt that this was going to be my night. However, there were still two more tables in play and as the game progressed and the blinds went forever higher the more skilful players gradually grinded me down and I didn't make it to the final table. However, I did learn something from this episode. I noticed that as the contest progresses the game takes on a different slant. It's alright being a little cautious and tight in the early rounds when the blinds are small, but it' a different ball game in the latter stages when the blinds are sky high. If you don't take chances you'll certainly be blinded out.

I'd been in Tasmania two months when I got my first win. As time passed I picked up on some of my mistakes and it appeared to pay off.

I discovered that Tasmania is well versed in playing poker and it is a popular pastime in cities like Launcesten, Burnie and Hobart. Consequently I signed up for competitions and played a few games in these places. I didn't fair too well at first and then luck was on my side. In total I won four tournaments and received my winnings along with some medals. I now felt like a high roller ... I was the king of the castle. My time in Tasmania was coming to an end and, my wife Elsina, and I, were about to fly back home to my home town, Burnley, England. I knew that the game was popular in Burnley because my nephew James is a keen poker player. I couldn't wait to get back home and skim a few pounds off my unsuspecting opponents. Little did I realise ... that my learning process was just about to begin.

CHAPTER 2 - BACK TO REALITY

I'd no sooner arrived back home in Burnley when I got in touch with my nephew James and asked him where the poker events took place.

"Alright Uncle John," he replied politely, "I always play every Thursday night at the Dugdale Arms and it starts at seven o'clock. However, there's another venue every Friday night at Reed and Simonstone Constitutional Club and that begins at eight o'clock, but I never go to that one."

"Thanks very much James ... I appreciate that, so God willing, I'll see you Thursday at the Dugdale."

"Cheers Uncle John ... I look forward to seeing you."

James was now in his fifties with two grown up daughters of his own and yet he was so respectful. It's funny really because in the next few months I was going to be tagged with the name 'Tas' as my poker name. This came about when the opponent sat next to me was John Nawab, and he was a fantastic poker player and very friendly.

"I'll tell you what John," he laughed, "seeing as you're from Tasmanian Devil country, your poker name from now on is Tas."

This created a laugh around the table but the funny part is that from that moment on the name stuck and I've been tagged with it ever since. James twigged onto my new nickname and one time during a game he approached me.

"Uncle John I hope you don't mind but is it alright to call you Tas like all the others do during the poker sessions."

"Aye of course it is James" I laughed, "and I appreciate you asking."

This he did and during the coming months I quickly realised what a good player he was.

One of the first gentlemen I met was Steve Wood and we hit it off from the word go. During the next two years we were to become firm friends. Unlike me, who had only been playing poker a short while, Steve was very experienced at the game. But we both had one thing in common ... we loved it and thought it was a magical game that brought all types of people together on level terms whether they were a millionaire or a bricklayer's labourer. Not only that ... we were both fascinated by how it is such an easy game to learn and yet so hard to master.

"How do you master this game Steve," I asked him one day.

"Hey John, that's one thing I can't tell you because it's nigh impossible. Nobody can give you a right strategy to play the game because, depending on the turn of the cards, anything can happen."

"I class myself as a passive player Steve ... do you think I should be more aggressive?"

"Well ... I can't really say. I've watched you playing and your strategy seems to be doing alright. Just keep playing the way you do and pick up on your mistakes. All I can say is there's a time to be passive and time to be aggressive."

That was the kind of banter that went on between us and one day he asked me if I was interested in writing a book about 'Texas Hold'em Poker'.

"U-um, I don't know Steve, there's a lot to writing a book ... where could I get all my material from?"

"You must be joking John ... there's all the different characters and many ups and downs of this crazy game. And not only that, millions of people all over the world are simply crazy about the game ... it'll be a best seller!"

"I thought about it for a minute before answering, "Aye, you may be right there Steve. I'll tell you what ... you join in the venture and I'll do it."

"Right, you're on," he said shaking my hand. From that moment on we were partners.

"To start the book off Steve I'm going to need a brief outline of your life so as to bring out your character.

A few days later he came to my house and gave me an account of his life and I found it to be, not only interesting, but also enlightening.

Steve was born in a Lancashire council house on 27th Aug 1951 and his childhood memories are of being cold and hungry. Due to poor living conditions his mother constantly suffered from ill health. His father was a very hard working man and regularly worked 12 hour shifts as a boiler man for Yates Engineering Firm. At weekend his dad would spend his leisure time chatting over a few pints of beer amongst his pub friends. He was usually strapped for cash but somehow he always managed to hire a car during Wake's Week and take his wife, son Steve and daughter Susan on a tour around Britain.

As a child Steve attended a catholic school and he hated every aspect of it. He couldn't stand the dogma and hated the strict, laid down doctrine and thought it was evil. It was during those schooldays that he had a sinister experience. He was only a small child and he had a strange uncanny sighting in the middle of the night. He lived in a small terraced house and from his bedroom window he had a clear view of Pendle Hill which, in the Middle Ages, was renowned for witchcraft and many a witch had been burnt at the stake. There were two single beds in the small bedroom ... one for him and one for his little sister.

He was normally a sound sleeper but, on this occasion, he was awoken by a strange eerie silence. His bedroom was in semi-darkness illuminated only by diffused light from the moon. As there were no noises within the room or outside he presumed it was after midnight. Then his senses reeled and he beheld an incredible vision. He thought at first he must be dreaming but a strange aroma in his nostrils told him otherwise. The silhouettes of five dark, eerie figures without any limbs glided smoothly across the room between the two beds towards the chimney breast. They were about three feet tall with just a head and a body. Even though they were black they had a transparent glow about them which made their countenance stand out. Then, lo and behold, he noticed another apparition with a tall mitre on its head. The ghost like figure was floating in a sitting position above the fireplace and the five transparent spectres seemed to be offering it gifts. Steve was terrified and tried calling his sister but she was sound asleep and didn't appear to hear him. Everything was clear for a few minutes and then in an instant they were gone, leaving the room tinged in greyness as, by now, only faint light emitted from a clouded moon.

Today, many years later, Steve has never again seen the apparition and yet it still affects his life. He is a talented artist and all his paintings appear to be of silhouettes against a glorious sunset. No matter how hard he tries, his paintings always appear to end up in the same vein. On reflection Steve thought it may be connected to the catholic dogma of going to hell fire if you're bad.

****

Consequently, he couldn't wait to leave school and his first job was as an apprentice motor mechanic in Accrington.

He settled into the job and enjoyed his new found freedom. Nevertheless, even though he was content, he had an overpowering urge to explore other pastures. He was determined to indulge into other ways of making money and he wasn't afraid to tackle anything. Keen as he was, work was hard to come by and this led him into breaking the law.   He and a friend called Alan, were found guilty at Preston Crown Court of stealing a car and burglary.   They were sentenced to three months in Buckley Hall, a young offender's institution in Rochdale. It had only just recently been opened and was one of the first of its kind in Great Britain. The scheme was designed to introduce a very strict and tough regime so as to deter offenders from ever wanting to go back there again.

"It certainly worked in my case," laughed Steve, "because I've never been a guest of Her Majesty since."

"Oh so it was rough in there was it Steve?"

"Rough! You can say that again ... it literally scared the crap out of me!"

"And were you guilty Steve?" I asked.

"I was certainly guilty of stealing the car but not the burglary, but I suppose it was my own fault."

"How come?"

"Well what it was ... as a boy I was always very mischievous. As I grew into my teens I got into a wrong crowd and ended up breaking the law. I didn't resent my mates or try to blame them as I had a mind of my own and openly knew the difference from right or wrong. I never did any burglaries or break in anywhere but a mate of mine called Roy did. On this particular occasion he broke into a church vicarage and stole some valuable items and Alan and I got the blame for it."

"You two got the blame .... how's that?"

"Well, like I've just said, it was my own stupid fault really because after Roy had broken into the vicarage I stupidly gave him permission to hide his booty in the very same garage where we'd hidden the stolen car and it wasn't long after that the police came and arrested me and Alan."

"You admit to stealing the car but how come you got done for burglary as well?"

"John, I didn't have much choice," he retorted, "you would have done the same. Back then in the sixties it was easy for the police to get a confession. I either signed the charge sheet or I finished up losing a mouthful of teeth ... I didn't fancy that."

"They scared you that much did they!"

"Too bloody true ... they scared the shit out of me. Anyway, the way I saw it there was an element of truth in it."

"How did the police get onto you?"

"Well, Roy was out one night in Blackburn with his girlfriend and he stupidly tried to sell some of his booty in a local cafe. Not long after that he was picked up by the police and they took him to the nick to help them with their enquiries."

"So he dropped you in it did he?"

"Aye he did, but I couldn't blame him for that. Like me ... he wanted to keep his teeth. And anyway, he may not have blabbed but his girlfriend Elaine, certainly did. She panicked when the police picked them up and openly gave them our addresses and willingly agreed to go to the police station to identify us as the ones totally responsible for everything."

"U-um, I take it you weren't very fond of her after that."

"Do you know something John ... it may seem strange but I actually felt sorry for her."

"Sorry for her ... how come?"

"Well what it is ... she was trying to protect her boyfriend Roy. She'd just recently been in a correction centre for young women and given birth to a baby boy whilst in there ... and Roy was the father. Her dad was a headmaster and her mother was also a teacher. They were strict disciplinarians and it didn't go down very well when the police arrived at their home with search warrants."

"That's good of you Steve ... you're very forgiving."

"Aye may be. But I'm glad I was because Roy left her and married someone else. Later on in life he murdered his wife and then hung himself on a gas lamp outside his home. Elaine never did get over him."

"It's all interesting stuff Steve but now tell me how you went on at Buckley Hall ... your new home?"

"My new home ... you must be joking! On entering the place it was a very frightening ordeal, I almost pissed myself. After laying down some ground rules and explaining us our rights, two guards ordered us to strip off and put on some prison uniforms. We were then frog marched to a cell where we were given some note paper and ordered to write home to our parents to say how well treated we were. On the first morning we were awoken by guards and ordered to stand to attention outside our cells. We'd only been there a short while when I heard a noise in the distance. The noise grew in intensity and got forever closer."

"What was it Steve?"

"It was a large group of young inmates running towards us in a line and as they passed by our cells each one gave us a sharp slap across our faces. I tried furiously to slap one or two of them back but it was nigh impossible as they rumbled so fast by us."

"By 'eck! I can imagine that was a bit daunting."

"A bit ... it was a bloody lot daunting. Anyway, I later found out that this is a ritual which all new prisoners go through on their first morning."

"Ha ha Steve ... a kind of welcoming committee."

"Yeah it may seem funny but I can assure you it wasn't funny at the time."

"Anyway, did you find out where the youngsters were marching off to?"

"Yeah we did and pretty quick at that. As soon as the last inmate had passed us the guards ordered us to follow. After propelling us along a balcony and down a flight of steel stairs we finished up in a large hall referred to as the 'Sock Room.' It was packed with young lads and they were all applying white powder to their feet prior to putting on clean socks. It turned out that this was a daily routine."

"I take it that you had to do the same?"

"Aye right in one. Anyway, as we were putting on our socks some of the boisterous youngsters approached us putting on a bravado act. A few did a spot of shadow boxing in front of us in an attempt to intimidate us."

"Did it scare you Steve."

"Too bloody well it scared me and it bloody well would have scared you as well."

"Aye, I'm sure it would. Anyway, did it settle down after a while?"

"Yeah it did. One of them asked me my name, where I was from and if I had any 'tics'."

"'Tics,'" I asked, what's a 'tic?"

"Well the lad just laughed at me, but I found out later that, in the criminal world, it was a kind of 'Badge of Honour'. The more tics you had meant you were a villain to be contended with."

"Ha ha," I laughed, "it must have scared you though because, like you said, you've been on the straight and narrow since then."

"It did that ... I certainly wouldn't like to go in there again."

****

After a brew Steve carried on with his tale. "After being released I had a go at being a farmhand, a landscape gardener, a grave digger, a milkman, a photographer and a

64

salesman. I took on anything trying to find my niche. I didn't settle too long in any of the above jobs but the experience gave me enough insight and confidence to set up my own business.

In the following years I set up a finance company, a National Video/Mobile Co-operation and even ran a taxi firm. To top it up I even took on another venture:

'STEPHEN WOOD'S PRIVATE INVESTIGATIONS'"

I couldn't help laughing. "All I can say Steve is God loves a trier."

"You can laugh John but doing all the different jobs was good experience and gave me a good deal of insight. I wasn't afraid to explore any avenue and eventually I became a tally man. I thoroughly enjoyed this aspect of my working life as I had young ladies working underneath me and also lots of my clients were of the opposite sex. It gave me a great opportunity to explore my carnal desires. Due to my success and affluence I somehow became much more attractive to the ladies and my sex life just exploded. I was a man of the world and sexual exploits were there for the taking and, to put it mildly, I took advantage of every opportunity that presented itself. The way I saw it, it was my duty to fulfil the sexual yearnings of any woman in need."

"Ha ha ... you were a bit of a randy bugger e-eh Steve?"

"I guess you could say that but then something happened to turn my world around. I had a good mate called Neville and we enjoyed many escapades together. He was married to a lady called Sue and they had three children, Roger, Duncan and Joanne. I too had a wife, and we had two children, Nichola and Kelly. Things were fine but then my wife Eileen began to suffer from post natal depression. Despite being a good loving wife and mother, she couldn't cope with all the motherly things in life. It took its toll and she spent several months in a mental health hospital. She became a different woman and, no matter how I tried, I couldn't get close to her. The condition didn't improve and, in her state of mind, she took out divorce proceedings against me. In the meantime, Neville, met and fell in love with a lady called Elaine. Susan, his wife, got to know about the affair and she divorced him."

"Oh I think I know what's coming now ... is Sue the same lady who's your partner now?"

"That's right John but let me explain how it came about. After my divorce I was left alone to bring up my two girls on my own. Luckily, my children and Sue's children still played with each other. In fact, Sue would take all the girls to ballet lessons together whilst I went about my business affairs. Things went on like this for a while and it gradually drew Sue and me closer together. We both realised that we'd fallen for each other and, on Jun 5th 1979, we decided to become an item. From that day forth I totally changed my way of life and became a very orientated family man ... Sue and the kids became my entire life. We've been extremely happy as a family unit ever since."

"So you finally decided to settle down eh? There's one thing for sure Steve ... you'd certainly sowed your wild oats before then."

"I did but I can honestly say that I put all that behind me."

"Were you still a tallyman at the time?"

"I was but one day, whilst out on my rounds, I got talking to Brian Healess, a customer, and he told me he had his own band called 'Studio 2000' which was going to play at a convention in Manchester in front of some renowned booking agents. I was rather sceptical but decided to go along to the gig and listen to his so called band. In my opinion, his band wasn't just good ... it was absolutely brilliant. The band was made up of Brian on guitar, Jon de Beth, the lead singer and two backing singers. They sang modern songs like 'Johnny Come Home,' but also some great songs that Brian had composed himself. Afterwards I asked him if he had a manager and he said no. 'You have now, I retorted with a grin on my face."

"Ah, so you were now into show business eh?"

"Well, like I mentioned earlier ... I wasn't afraid to take on anything. I soon realised that Brian was the brains behind the outfit. He founded the band, wrote the songs and played lead guitar. He also recorded drums and other instruments which he used as backing tapes during each performance. I've got to admit that Jon de Both was a brilliant singer but, the problem was that he knew it and thought way beyond his station. Hence, he wanted more control over the band and how to run things. He was an ex-professional singer having performed in Dubai, Ireland and other places. He'd also been a contestant on 'Opportunity Knocks' and pointed out that he was likened to a French crooner. The artistic difference between Brian and Jon caused friction amongst the band and, as Jon didn't get his own way, he decided to go solo."

"Oh, a bit of a knock back then ... did that bother you?"

"It did a bit but I realised that Brian was a good singer in his own right but needed a bit of an image change. By the time I had finished with him he had a totally different persona. I had him performing in a black rimmed hat with a leather headband, strumming a white Stratocaster guitar with a leather studded strap. His new stage name was Brian Healess, all the way from Queens in New York. I thought this was funny and really bizarre, as he was a lad from Accrington, a typical Lancashire cotton mill working town.   When Jon left the act he took his wife Louise, who was one of the backing singers, with him.   That's when my stepson Roger, joined the act.   He happened to be a student at the time and wanted to promote his college band, VICIOUS.   He didn't fancy doing cabaret but I persuaded him that the experience would enhance his chances of performing at the St George's Hall in Blackburn."

"VICIOUS, was it a punk band?"

"No, he was more into pop music.   But on saying that, the name of his band did cause quite a commotion at one event which I organised."

"Oh this sounds interesting ... tell me more!"

"Well, I arranged for four of my acts to perform at the Plough Inn in Great Harwood and it was like a mini Glastonbury.   The acts consisted of a Beatles tribute with a female drummer --- Kym Marsh --- VICIOUS and a trio that did Gary Numan covers."

"Who's Gary Numan?"

"He's an English singer, songwriter, composer who also produces records; he was the front man for the new wave band 'Tubeway Army'.   His debut album, Pleasure Principle, was released in September 1979 and it peaked at Number one in the United Kingdom."

"Oh right ... I vaguely remember his name. Anyroad, back to what you were saying, what caused the commotion?"

"Well all the acts went down well until my band VICIOUS, went onto the stage. I think the crowd was expecting some vile punk offensive music and, from the onset, they started throwing missiles at the act. This obviously agitated the band and they in turn began to throw missiles back. The tension escalated to the point where an angry mob started to make death threats. It cooled down a little but when the band attempted to leave the stage a rowdy crowd sealed them off. 'Right that's enough!' I bawled as I bull-nosed my way to the front. Back in those days I was a white Mike Tyson and I warned them to fuck off or I would murder them. I had a reputation that preceded me of keeping a stack of rifles and eight rottweilers in my home. The situation calmed down a little but then erupted again. An angry rabble gathered outside the dressing room trapping all the performers inside. After a phone call a rival gang, Blackburn Youth, turned up and all hell broke loose. Talk about a gangster film ... this was for real. Skinheads hurled pint glasses and other objects through the air. One lad got hit over the head with a glass and another got one smashed in his face. During the skirmish there was blood and spit all over the place.

Women fled the scene by escaping through fire doors and over high garden fences or any other possible route. The fracas went on until a squadron of police turned up and arrested many of the offenders. It was only then that the Vicious could safely leave the building. The band received death threats for a while after that, but I never received any."

"Did this incident mar your enthusiasm for the music business at all?

"Well it did a bit but I thought sod it! From that moment on I decided if I was going to take it on I would do it big time. Hence, I took on other bands as well and forged forward into the unknown. It cost me a mint as I made sure that my bands were well equipped with the finest equipment that money could buy. And it wasn't just musical instruments that I supplied but also the best lighting and sound effects. It was a lot of expenditure but it paid off. Word spread around that my bands were good and I soon had agents across the country contacting me."

"Good, this is becoming interesting; where did you go from here?"

"Well, the incident at the Plough Inn became notorious but, luckily, it didn't sully my image. In fact, the publicity actually brought me to the fore and enhanced my reputation. In order to promote my acts I got a good booking at King George's Hall in Blackburn, a venue renowned for its famous bands. Prior to my contract date a unique musical festival had been organised at the venue for 'Gigs of the Eighties.' For the experience I took two of my acts, Vicious and JB Healess, of Studio 2000 along with me to watch them. On reaching the venue it was an eye opener as a rowdy mob gathered around the ticket office and it was clear that they were out to cause trouble. They were obviously fans of 'The Mac Lads,' a band from Macclesfield who were one of the acts. Lots of them were tooled up with Stanley knives, kitchen knives, coshes and any other weapon they could disguise within their clothing. Luckily, lots of security men were on their toes and readily aware of what was going on. These dickheads or so-called fans were using the festival solely as an excuse for hooliganism."

"Oh I think I know what's coming ... is it another incident like at the Plough Inn?"

"Well you could say that except that this was twice as bad. The first act was a support act called, 'Then Jericho,' a rock band that had slight fame in the eighties with the song, Muscle Deep. They'd also performed on 'Top of the Pops' and had four top 40 hits in the UK. Nevertheless, despite their reputation, they were badly matched in this situation. They'd no sooner started to play than a rowdy rabble at the front of the stage started to spit and hassle them. The band tried to play it down but it was useless; it became obvious that the mob was only interested in listening to The Macc Lads. Then Jericho never got to finish its act, but they were only to pleased to leave the stage."

"U-um, I vaguely remember them playing on Top of the Pops."

"Yeah, so do I. Anyway, prior to the entrance of The Macc Lads, six roadies cordoned off the stage with a large wooden barrier in order to protect the act from impending attack. I was informed later that this was standard procedure wherever they performed. The Mac Lads came onto the stage and they were self proclaimed as the rudest, crudest, drunkest and vilest band in Christendom. Their foul mouths and politically incorrect lyrics were connected with binge drinking, sex and fighting. I'm no angel but, in my opinion, they were not only terrible ... they were downright disgusting. Their act was repulsive in every sense of the word and yet, their fans loved it ... it was abhorrent!"

"Aye, I've never heard them but my son Craig, who is a musician, told me that they are vile and completely rubbish."

"And he's right too. As they entered the stage there was a loud roar of approval from the huge crowd. The band had only been playing its vile music for about ten minutes when hysteria exploded into a frenzy. The sound system was by far superior to the previous one and loud music vibrated around the room causing the crazy crowd to ramp up and start moshing and jumping up and down like halfwits. In their insanity they deliberately collided with other dancers. Tension built up and hard core nutters wreaked havoc and chaos throughout the entire venue. People were packed together like sardines in the great hall and I can only describe it as a mosh pit. Thugs immersed within the crowd and started to incite them by kicking and lashing out. My bands and I were stood in what I thought was a safe area but a thug came too close for comfort. Bang! I swung a right punch that landed square on the dickhead's chin and laid him out. He was just one of many others who were lying on the floor. Parading bouncers picked them up by the scruff of their necks and escorted them from the building."

"It's happen as well there were plenty of bouncers around."

"You're not kidding, it were like bedlam in there. As the gig progressed the spitting became so intense that gunge was hanging from the band's guitars and faces like honeysuckle. It appeared even more disgusting because the band incited the rowdy crowd for more of the nasty sickening drivel. Then thugs, amongst the crowd, started to hurl chairs and other missiles over the barrier onto the stage. A projectile broke a stage lighting and glass crashed down onto the band's heads. Hired heavies moved in to drive the rowdies away from the stage and the band carried on. The Macc Lads got through their act and, by the grace of God, nobody was killed. But there were quite a lot of casualties and I'm sure the A&E were kept busy that night."

"By 'eck Steve, did it not make you think twice about bringing your acts to this venue?"

"Did it hell as like. In fact, it got me to thinking of all the publicity something like this brings to whatever band is playing."

"That's all right but isn't it bad publicity?"

"John, there's an old expression quoted by P T Barnum, a 19th century American showman and circus owner ... 'There's no such thing as bad publicity.' I did no more but book several of my acts into the next forthcoming venue. Vicious was the main act but I also included Studio 2000, the Gary Numan tribute, and many others. Before the event, of all places, we had a band meeting at the Plough Inn to air our views. I had large format posters placed around different towns in prominent places and I placed an advert in the Lancashire Evening Telegraph. The add read that my band Vicious made The Macc Ladds look like girls. The clippings caused a lot of hostility and hatred amongst the

75

local dickheads and, even before the gig, the death threats started up again."

"Did you not think you were reaping up trouble?"

I did but I threw caution to the wind. The way I saw it was that the adverse publicity would bring in lots of dough."

"That's all right Steve but what about all the thugs that you were aware off ... did you build a barrier across the stage like they did for The Macc Lads?"

"Ha ha, for security I hired a few bouncers and I also called upon some of my hardest mates who owed me a favour. I asked them to make their presence known by standing at each side of the stage. Also, anyone with weapons or the wrong face was turned away at the entrance by security men. All of my life's experiences and streetwise tactics helped to make my venture a success. The venue was packed to capacity with well over 1000 tickets sold."

"So you packed them in Steve but, how did the show go down?"

"Well it was a bit iffy at the start but overall it was a great success. Each act got to do a fifteen minute spot of fame and was well received. However, due to the adverse publicity, Vicious was rather nervous and needed a few bevvies to calm down their nerves before they performed.

Hence, their act was a bit messy in parts and one of the players fell backwards onto a drum kit whilst another got in the way of a pyrotechnic and finished up with a face full of black gunpowder. Unsettled spectators started to heckle them and throw missiles. Nevertheless, when the band recovered its composure and began to play good musical sounds, the audience realised they were good and started to calm down, It became obvious that, although they were a bit intoxicated, they were not at all like The Macc Lads. Consequently, the gig went down very well and a good night was enjoyed by all. At the end of the show, an encore was requested, and all the bands joined together on the stage and sang and danced in harmony."

"I take it you were happy with the outcome?"

"Too true I was. It turned out to be a success story as I had hired two cameramen to film the entire show. After scrutinising the film I edited it and used it as a promotional video to showcase all of my acts. Hence, from then onwards, my bands had loads of work in famous working men's clubs and other prestigious functions. My little enterprise prospered extremely well and I set up a recording studio and called it 'HOLLYWOOD INCORPERATION'. It was a great success and, in the nineties, I became the manager of many bands and solo artists. My company grew and can only be described as AN EXPLOSION OF THE NINETIES."

"Ha ha, did you live up to the reputation?"

"Well, being an entrepreneurial business man I had to dress the part and I had a great wardrobe. But I didn't follow fashion and always did my own thing and was rather flamboyant. I bought expensive Italian suits and patent brogues. I was quirky and wore Jesus sandals and red socks."

"Ha ha, so you had an air of panache about you eh?"

"You can laugh John but, even though I was rather outlandish, I took the music business very seriously. I was once employed as a newspaper photographer in the Isle of Man, and I used my photographic skills in a photo shoot so as to promote Studio 2000 and enhance their image. My idea was to create images which could be used in post-production or editing. Technology back then in the 80's wasn't geared up like nowadays and I had to do more than 200 shots before I came up with the right photo. I printed the final image on an A4 sheet with autographs. Surprisingly they went down like a bomb and there was a great demand for them."

"So all the effort you put in paid off?

"Yeah, in fact, success was building up and that's when I decided to open a recording studio in Great

Harwood. I recorded demo acts to a professional standard and promoted them. Many people from far and wide came to the studio in order to record their songs and get some representation."

"Were any of them successful?"

"Aye, course they were ... have you heard of Kym Marsh?"

"Do you mean her off Coronation Street?"

Yeah, she's the one. I know she's an actress but she was a singer and a songwriter as well. In 2001, she won a place on Popstars with the band Hear Say."

"U-um, I remember listening to her ... she had a nice voice."

And then there was Jarvis Cocker ... he was really talented but nobody took him serious back then. I've got to admit John, I made a big mistake with him. He came to me for an audition and I turned him down flat. At that particular time I'd had a load of knock backs from different agents and I was feeling a little down in the mouth. After the audition I actually turned to him and told him to give up music and look for another job. He not only became a famous musician, he became a famous actor and presenter as well. He later became the founder, front man, lyricist and solo consistent member of the band Pulp. Following Pulp's hiatus he pursued a solo career and, for seven years, he presented the BBC Radio Music Show ... 'Jarvis Cocker's Sunday Service'. He then became a figurehead of the Britpop genre in the mid 1990's."

"What's a Britpop group?"

"Well basically they were groups that based their music mainly from British pop groups of the 1960's, punk of the 1970's and indie of the 1980's. Their music and culture emphasised Britishness. Most of the groups were instrument based, with guitars being a big focus for a lot of bands. They produced brighter, catchier alternative rock sound, as opposed to the darker styles of the US grunge music. Britpop tradition was to play easy to listen to guitar music, in a similar vein to that of the Beatles and the Rolling Stones ... it was about songs, guitars, jackets and attitudes. It took elements of guitar rock and pop music to create a new genre of rock."

"By 'eck Steve, Jarvis Cocker did really well for himself. All I can say is that you made one big bloomer not taking him on."

"Aye, and don't I know it ... don't remind me!"

"Not to worry eh ... taking everything into account you seemed to be doing okay."

"Yeah I was but at one time I had a little problem with the police."

"Oh don't say that ... you mentioned earlier that you didn't fancy being a guest of Her Majesty ever again."

"Oh it wasn't like that. A particular police constable turned up at my studio and kept asking me leading questions. He obviously thought I was up to something illegal. He may have been following a lead but it got to the point where he was turning up in civvy clothes when he was off duty. One day I'd had enough and instinctively kicked him in the bollocks. He threatened that I was in serious trouble but, thankfully, nothing came of it."

"Oh so everything is not as rosy as it appears in the music game."

"Too right it's not. Expenses was another problem. My overall expenditure was massive and, as none of my acts were under contract to a recording company, my funds were running low. I had to consort to other means of balancing the books. One short term solution was to contract Studio 2000 to play a ten day stint for the British Army in Germany in front of the troops. It solved a bit of my money problems but then, along came another one. The band complained that they were over worked and under paid. When I couldn't meet their demands they resorted to boycotting the last two gigs of the contract. Being a hard nosed business man I made it clear that they would not only be out of a job but it would also culminate in the end of the band. On saying this, I always strived to put the interest of the band at heart and to fulfil their requests. Even to the point of wiping their arses and believe you, me ... it was no easy task."

"Ha ha, that's one way of putting it Steve! Just one more question ... how secure was all the valuable equipment that you had in your studio?"

"Good question. At one time rumour came to my attention that someone was planning to break into the Studio and steal anything of value they could. Hence, I left four rottweilers on the property overnight. The next morning I found a broken snooker cue and a trail of blood that led down a flight of stairs. Nothing of value was missing and, although someone may have easily broken into the studio, they certainly had a hard time leaving it."

****

Alas, all the stress and toil of business along with Steve's hectic lifestyle began to take its toll. He began to feel ill and went to see his GP. The doctor advised him to change his lifestyle.

Steve did this in a dramatic way. He closed down the studio and gave away all of his assets and decided to go into voluntary work. He threw himself into his new project and one of his tasks was to take aid to orphanages in Romania. The episode opened his eyes to the suffering of others and it touched him deeply. From then onwards he made a pledge to make voluntary work his life's work.

But then the INLAND REVENUE got onto him and didn't believe he'd given everything away. To get them off his back he took a job working for Hyndburn Borough Council as a dog warden. Incidentally this job had a direct bearing on his future life. His task was to pick up abandoned stray dogs and take them to a local compound. He liked this aspect of the job but there was one thing he didn't like at all. He'd pick up dogs and take them to the compound only to find out that most of the dogs he'd taken there the week before were being put to sleep. He couldn't believe it ... he was completely mortified. He felt like packing the job in there and then but decided otherwise.

"No," he thought to himself, "I'll stay here a bit longer and find out as much as I can about all the procedures, and maybe I will be able to help these poor animals."

This he did and in the meantime he got in touch with The Powers That Be, and enquired if he could set up a charity for the welfare of stray dogs.

The curt reply from the council was "Yes, that's alright as long as it does not cost us anything."

To Steve, a nod was as good as a wink; he didn't need telling twice. From that moment on he, along with his family, started up a charity.

HYNDBURN STRAY DOGS IN NEED

To their credit, Steve and his family put lots of effort and love into this wonderful venture and it became a great success. From that day forward many a dog's life was saved and cherished. Over the next few years the charity won many awards and in 2009 Steve was deservedly awarded:

DOG WARDEN OF THE YEAR.

The charity is still going strong today.

I always thought that Steve was a gentleman but, after listening to his life-story I knew this was a man to be respected and I feel honoured to work alongside him in our new venture,

******

Whilst chatting to Steve he enlightened me about an incident, which occurred in the city of Oradea, Romania, and it was far more terrifying than his time spent in Buckley Hall as a youth.

It truly was a frightening experience, and this is what he related to me:

"It was Aug 1995 and there was an article in the Daily Mirror newspaper. John Boast, a mate of mine, had 2 years previously been arrested in Romania on a charge of kidnapping babies from an orphanage and then laundering them out to rich clients from various countries. However, John pleaded not guilty to the charges. His only action was assisting couples to legally adopt babies from the orphanage after background checks had been carried out by British Social Services. I know him only too well and I can vouch that he is a man of good character with good morals. I truly believed him to be innocent. The article in the newspaper stated how corrupt the Romanian government was. Despite his plea of innocence, John had already served 2 years in appalling conditions awaiting trial and there was no prospect of that in the near future. The article went on to say that I was flying out there to try and bail him out financially and to plead for him. My wife, Sue, was against the idea but, because she knew I was determined to go, she decided to come along and support my venture."

"And when did you realise you were treading on dangerous grounds Steve?"

"Pretty quick I can assure you. In fact it was on our first day there. I'd already booked an appointment with a lady solicitor and we arrived at her office at about 11am. Not being able to speak the language I had hired an interpreter called Emile. The lady had a very stern serious face and she handed me an unopened letter that was from John. On reading the letter my heart sank into my stomach as I began to realise the gravity of my situation. I just sat there with my head in my hands and my face must have turned to 10 shades of grey. I not only felt sick for myself but also for the dangerous position that I had put my wife, Sue, into."

"Cor, blimey! What did the letter say?"

"Basically it was a warning and John was cautioning me not to, under any circumstances, come to Romania. It stated that if I went to the police station I would immediately be arrested and put in Jail. Because I had been mentioned in the newspaper clipping I would be charged with aiding and abetting the crime and I would have no rights whatsoever. By my reaction to the letter it was obvious to everyone that something was wrong."

Oh 'eck Steve, you'd got yourself into a right predicament hadn't you? I can imagine how you felt because the culture over there is corrupt and the language barrier would have complicated things."

"Oh that wasn't the end of it. Like I said, the lady solicitor was very serious but after realising the contents of the letter her whole countenance changed. She became edgy, frustrated and appeared frightened. She just beckoned to the door and asked us to leave. As it happened, the police station where John was confined was just across the street from the law firm and could be seen from the office window. As we left the building a lot of uniformed police and soldiers were parading the street carrying weapons. I had a white suit on sporting a white trilby ... I stood out like a soar thumb. It was a totally terrifying experience and I was absolutely crapping myself."

"So what did you do ... did you make your way back to your digs?"

"No, did I bloody hell ... I just wanted to get away from there as fast as possible. I asked Emile to drive us to the border so we could cross over into Hungary. He wasn't very happy about it but he was persuaded when I offered him a hefty tip."

"Yeah, that seems to work all over the world."

"Anyway, after a long anxious trip we luckily passed through both the Romanian customs and the Hungary sector as well into a small town called Szolnoc."

"Ah well you must have felt a lot better now that you were in a different country."

"No. you're wrong there John. Sue and I were still on tenterhooks as we felt that we may be apprehended at any moment and deported back to Romania."

"How long were you in Szolnoc?"

"Just a few days but after paying our hotel bill and the train fare to Budapest we'd run out of cash. The cost of a plane fare back to London was £600 each. Luckily we had one travel cheque left. When we landed in London our only possessions were the clothes we stood up in. We felt rather dishevelled but were eternally grateful to be back on British soil. We were skint but luckily a good friend, Roy Baker, came all the way from Lancs and picked us up."

The story did have a happy ending because shortly afterwards, John's case came to the fore and he was found not guilty because of lack of evidence against him.

****

Reflecting back to my first night's venue in the Dugdale Arms where I'd initially met Steve I got sat around a table ready for my first game of poker in England.

The venue was run by Darren Yates, a local man, who was helped by his lady-friend Colette. I soon learned that Darren's poker name was Daz. The format was slightly different to the one in Tasmania but still pliable. The starting stack was 7000 chips and the price was thirteen pounds. But, three pounds of this went into a two pots. One pot was for attaining a straight flush and the other was for a **royal flush.**

The pots would build up over the weeks until someone came up with either a straight or a Royal flush. If a player won with one holding card in his hand he would only get half of the pot but with two holding cards he would scoop up the lot. Obviously a Royal flush is much harder to achieve and the pot was usually much higher. Another pot was set aside for a league which ran over three months and cash prizes were given out to 1st, 2nd and 3rd places. The competition usually consisted of up to forty players and to organise such an event is no easy task. However, Darren and his partner Colette, do a marvellous job.

The blinds started at 25/50 and increased every fifteen minutes until a break at eight o'clock. Now if anyone lost all their chips before the break they were allowed to re-buy a 5000 stack for ten pounds. During the break players could purchase an 'add on' of 7000 chips for ten pounds. Anyone with a stack of 2500 or less was allowed to purchase a re-buy and an add on. But, after the break there was no more buying ... it was now strictly at the knock out stage.

Now happy with the course of events I gazed around the room and, just like in Tasmania, there were people from many different walks of life. There were 36 players set up on four tables. On my table were nine players. My first encounter going clockwise around the table was Andrew, an accomplished builder and landlord. It became easy to remember Andrew as he was forever going All In even with basic holding cards. I noticed that he went All In blind on the very first hand.

"I can't believe what you've just done Andrew," I quipped, "you haven't even looked at your cards yet."

"Aye, it's right enough," he laughed, "I like to make things interesting and build up a big pot"

"That's alright but anyone with a decent starting hand is sure to take you on."

"That's what I want," he replied with a smile on his face, "I'm willing to take the risk because I like to build my stack up in the early stages."

I could understand his logic but I didn't go along with it. Nevertheless I couldn't believe what happened next. Two players took him on and one had pocket Aces. On turning his cards over Andrew had 2/7 and finished up with two small pair and won the hand.

"Ah-h, that's better," he gloated as he scooped up well over 21000 chips, "now I can relax a little."

"Well it takes all kinds," I thought as I picked up my next holding cards. Consequently, Andrew was tagged with the nickname 'All In Andrew.'

Next to Andrew was Lionel, a very friendly gentleman from Barbados of Afro-Caribbean descent. He had long dark plaited hair way below his shoulders and laughed heartily showing pearly white teeth. At least I thought he was friendly until later on in the game he took all my chips off me. In months to come I was to get my revenge but it was all taken in good fun. As mentioned earlier, it's only a game but every player I know yearns to win.

Bill was the next player in line and he was a canny player if I ever saw one. Like Darrel in Tasmania, he always seemed to get the upper hand over me when I fronted up to him. He was Lionel's mate and he lived in Great Harwood.

Next in line was my nephew James and I soon realised he was a rather aggressive player. But his tactics seemed to work and he soon had a nice stack of chips in front of him.

My next encounter was Irish John and he was always a bit strapped for cash, but he made up for this by his success at the table. Me myself, I'm never too sure what to do when I pick up pocket Aces. I don't know whether it's wise to hang back or go on the offensive. Irish John doesn't give it a second thought ... his tactic is to attack aggressively so as to scare players into folding and not giving them an opportunity to hit a flush, a straight or even two pairs. He's probably right because I've come unstuck many a time by holding back.

Sat beside him was his girlfriend Vicky, a gorgeous girl and nice with it. I liked both of them from the word go but I couldn't understand why they constantly wanted to fleece me of my chips. In the coming months I was to go along with John & Vicky to a gigantic tournament called the Goliath, in Coventry. The venue was held in a great hall as big as a supermarket and there were hundreds of tables. Running in conjunction with the contest was another venue called 'Joker's Wild' and there were more than 500 entrants ... and first prize was £9000. Believe it or not Vicky ended up in the last ten and she was, by far, the chip leader. They decided to split the pot and most competitors ended up with £1500. But as Vicky, had more than double the amount of chips than anyone else, she walked away with £3000 ... it was a nice start to the weekend.

Sat next to Vicky was Luggy and what a character he is. He is now in his fifties but is quite disabled due to the side effects of diabetes and a mild stroke. Disabled or not, he is very outspoken and boisterous with a vocabulary of his own, and every body knows when Luggy is around. He is a character on his own and loves chatting about his young life when he was fit and strong and openly boasts he could handle himself. Nowadays, due to a mild stroke, he is down on his uppers a little and readily admits that Thursday night poker is the highlight of his week.

Next to Luggy was Phil, another businessman who runs a factory over in Nelson. Phil is a very friendly man and he often holds poker sessions in his beautiful home. A poker table is set up in a huge double garage and he puts on all kinds of goodies. I've got to say he is the perfect host.

Finally to my right was Steve, smartly dressed and wearing a hat.

"I like your hat," I commented.

"Yeah it's for carrying my stack of chips to the final table," he laughed.

As I gazed around the table it once again it dawned on me, just like it had done in Tasmania, that this superb game of Texas Hold'em poker is a great social gatherer ... the way it brings people of all walks of life together is magical.

After introductions the game got under way and as mentioned, Andrew won the first hand by going All In blind. As the game progressed I guess you could call me a tight player ... I like to think that I am careful. I won and lost a few hands and by the break I had built up to 15,000 thousand chips. During the break I bought an add-on and so started the knock out session with 22000 chips. I was doing alright until I picked up Q/J and the flop was 9/Q/J. I was first to go and I bet 3000. A few players folded and then it came around to Lionel and he raised it to 8000. All the others folded and it came back to me. I felt confident that I had him and called. The turn card was a three and so I bet another 5000. Not only did he call me but he went 'All In'. I didn't read the table cards as I should have done and I also made the mistake of chasing the chips I had already put into the pot. Without giving it too much thought I called the shot and to my dismay, Lionel had K/10 which gave him a straight. My only chance was another Queen or Jack but it wasn't meant to be. Lionel gleefully scooped up all the chips. Like I mentioned earlier ... "I thought he liked me!" Joking aside we shook hands and we've been good buddies ever since.

Well that was my first session at the Dugdale Arms and I finished twelfth out of thirty two.

"A-ah, not too bad I suppose," I mused as I drove home, "better luck next time."

That was my first and last session at the Dugdale Arms because Daz changed venues and all future games were held at the Ighten Leigh Club.

Next evening, still keen to follow up on my new found hobby, I made my way to Read and Simonstone Constitutional Club. On arriving there I met up with some known faces, Steve, Bill, Lionel and All In Andrew. As it happened there was another Andy there, Andy Holt, and he was a multi millionaire, who owns Accrington Stanley Football Club. He also ran a large engineering firm on an industrial estate. He may be a millionaire but he is such a genuine nice down to earth bloke. When Andy is playing poker he is just one of the lads.

The bloke who ran the game, Mark, is also quite affluent, but without any airs and graces at all. On my table were two Peters and both of them were friendly retired gentlemen. One was a rather big man and got tagged with the nickname Big Pete. Sat next to Big Pete was Lee and he turned out to be a very canny player and hard to beat. The final player was Michael, an affluent bloke who spent most of the winter in Thailand.

Looking around I noticed a lot of younger people and they were all keen on the game. Teenagers, retired gentlemen, builders and business millionaires all brought together by a common denominator ... Texas Hold'em Poker. What a remarkable game!

The format was different again and I liked it. The buy in price was twenty pounds for 16000 chips but, once you got down to 8000 chips or below, you could re-buy another 16000 for ten pounds. I liked this aspect of it as I felt more confident with having more chips. Just like at the Dugdale Arms the starting blinds were 25/50 and they went up every fifteen minutes. At the break you were allowed to buy in another 16000 chips no matter how high your stack was. Players with fewer than 8000 chips were allowed to purchase 32000 more. After the break it was knockout time and no one could purchase any more.

A pot was set aside for anyone who achieved a straight flush.

The game commenced and in the first half I didn't win a single hand. It wasn't that I was being cautious ... I hardly got good holding cards and when I did I didn't get any follow up cards. However, after the break, luckily for me, Lady Luck came to the rescue and I started to win a few hands. Down to ten players I was lucky enough to take a player out and I landed on the final table with a nice healthy stack of chips. In only the first hand I came heads up with Mark. I had A/K and the flop was A/K/2. Mark bet 4000 and I raised him to 8,000. He stared at me warily and paused before calling. The turn card was 6 and there was no chance of a flush. He stared at me again and then bet another 4000. I weighed up the table cards and this time I raised him to 10000. Once again he gave me that deep stare trying to weigh me up. He'd never come across me before and I suppose he thought I may be bluffing. He hung on a little while more and then decided to fold. I was relieved because, even though I felt I had him, my mind went back to when I had been stung before.

The night turned out well for me. I didn't win the bout because Big Pete and Lionel asked if we could split the pot. I was happy with that as I went home around £140 in profit.

As I drove home my confidence was sky high and I felt as though I was to become a player to be reckoned with. Alas, my opponents didn't seem to take kindly to my line of thought and let me know in no uncertain ways.

The following Thursday evening at the Dugdale I was sat on the main table where Daz sat. I call it the main table because, as Daz organised everything he always sat in the same place so that he could take money and dish out chips whenever necessary. Another reason for calling it the main table is because it always ended up as the final table.

After just a few hands I picked up pocket Aces. I immediately thought about Irish John's strategy of being aggressive, but then decided to play my own style. I'd 9000 chips in front of me and Luggy bet 1000 and Daz called. Rather than raise it I played passive and just called. Others folded leaving just three of us. The flop came and it was A/8/8.

"Wow," I thought ... a full house Aces up!"

Luggy was first to go and he bet 2000. Daz studied for a while and then muttered, "Oh why not?" and then called.

Now it was my turn and I was in a bit of a quandary. I didn't want to frighten them off and so I just called.

The turn card produced a J and to my delight Luggy went all in. To enhance my pleasure Darren went all in as well. I couldn't believe my luck ... there was now over

18000 chips in the pot. With confidence I called with my remaining chips eager to pick up my winnings.

Unfortunately, my arrogance was soon brought crashing down to earth. On the turn of cards, Luggy had A/J and Darren had pocket eights ... four of a kind. I couldn't possibly win on the river because Luggy had the other Ace. What a come down ... it left me and Luggy with no option but to go for a buy in. It was yet another hard learning experience for me.

****

I hadn't been playing the game very long and my overall performance demonstrated this. So I took to reading poker books about how to improve my game. One tip I picked up was to be more vigilant of the table cards and another was the advantage of my position. I usually made my decision quickly but on my next session I was determined to study each situation carefully. There were eight players on the table and sat directly to my right was Irish John. Of all the players in the club, John is my nemesis. No matter what hand I get he always seems to come out on top.

"Never mind," I thought, "at least I bet after him."

The hands progressed and the blinds were 2000/4000 and it happened be my deal. I had a stack of

25500 chips. The first player, Steve, raised to 8000 and two others, including Irish John, called the bet.

My starting cards were 8/9 of hearts. It wasn't a premium hand but as the dealer, I had the advantage of seeing all the action take place before it reached me. I'd also recently read that medium-size suited cards can sometimes pay dividends if they connect.

"Oh 'eck!" I said to myself, "In for a penny in for a pound."

Small blind folded and the big blind called. The flop was K/7hearts 6/clubs. It was a little encouraging as I had flush draw and also an open-ended straight. Big blind bet a 4000 and the Steve re-raised to 8000 and the next player folded. John paused for a while and then flat calls the 8000. Testing my new theory I tried to figure out what the hell was going on. The best possible hand anyone could have at that moment was a set of kings. But I discounted that as I felt they would have raised the bet before the flop. Still, one of them may have a set of 6s or 7s. I also discounted anyone on A/4hearts because I thought they would have tried to end the hand there and then with a big raise. I wasn't sure but I put one of them on a pair of kings with a big kicker. Taking my number of outs into consideration I decided to call. Big blind studied a little and decided to fold leaving just

Steve, John and myself. To my delight the turn was 5/diamonds.

"Oh great!" I thought, "Up to now I've got the nuts ... I can't be beat. The only thing to do now is to capitalise on this divine gift."

I was surprised to see both Steve and John simply check. I suspected that Steve was slow playing and setting a trap so as to induce a bet and then raise the stakes. I concluded that John was onto Steve's game and maybe doing something similar. Normally, in this kind of situation, I would have gone All In there and then to end the hand but then I got greedy. I bet 4000 to make it look as though I was trying to steal the pot. My idea was that Steve or John would check raise me and then I could go in for the kill. But my greed didn't pay off ... both players just flat called. In short, I'd just missed a great opportunity to end the hand and scoop up the pot. Then came the river card and it was Q/hearts ... it was a card I didn't want to see even though my hand had improved from a straight to a flush.

Steve shook his head, tutted a little, and simply checked. That was a good sign but then it came to John's turn. He studied the table cards for what seemed an age. He then turned to me, smiled and asked me the only question I didn't want to hear.

"Alright Tas ... how many chips have you got in front off you?"

He then called All In covering both mine and Steve's tally of chips.

"You dopey Bastard!" I muttered to myself as I felt the colour draining out of my face. I realised what a quandary I had put myself into as now. I knew only too well that my flush could be beaten. I'd left myself cast out to sea in a boat without a paddle. The pot was over 70000 which left me no choice other than too call his bet.

"Too much for me," said Steve pushing his cards into the middle of the table.

On the turn of cards John had J/4hearts and he happily scooped up his reward. I had no option but to put it down to experience and go to the toilet with my tail between my legs and have a good cry. As stated previously, Irish John definitely is my nemesis.

****

During the following weeks I fared quite well at Read but I couldn't seem to do anything at the Ighten Leigh Club. Then, strangely enough, on my eightieth birthday I reached the final table and finished up head to head with my nephew James. We decided to split the pot and leave just £30 on the table and play on for league points. He had a slight edge on me in chips but it kept swinging back and forth until he went All In before the flop and my holding cards were A/J.

I thought about it for a little while and mumbled to myself, "Oh 'eck .... why not, I'll not get a much better chance than this."

It turned out he had pocket 9's and they carried him right through to the river.

I was a little disappointed and yet happy ... I had broken my duck at the Dugdale.

It turned out to be true because two weeks later I won the event outright. Mind you I had Lady Luck riding on my side. Just previously Daz had added another caption to the event and called it 'The Bounty.' The idea was for players to pay an extra £5 and they were in the 'Bounty'. Usually about twenty players opted for it meaning there was a pot of £100. Everyone's name, who had paid, was put into a hat. At the break a draw was made and whoever's name came out of the hat was the Bounty and he received £25. The idea was to try and knock out the Bounty and win the remaining £75.

On this occasion Daz happened to be the Bounty. I had favourable cards that night and I gradually reached the final table and Daz was still in the game. My game plan worked well and I finished in the last four and Daz was one of them. The prize money for the last four was £240 - £180 - £110 - £50. I wasn't the chip leader but I still had enough chips to knock Daz out and win the Bounty. This is when luck came into play. I was big blind and Daz followed me. My holding cards were A/2 suited and Darren went All In. The other two players folded leaving it up to me."

I studied it for a while and my thought's went back to when he'd beaten my full house Aces up with quad 4's.

However, I did decide to call for two reasons: number one, I had a chance of making a nut flush and number two, I could steal the bounty.

"Yeah, why not" I mumbled to myself, " I've got fifty quid in the sack no matter what happens and if I take him out I pocket £185."

This is where Lady Luck came and sat down beside me. "Yeah righto Daz," I said warily, "I call you!"

On the turn of cards he had A/J and the sequence of events went as follows:

7/9/4 on the flop. 10 on the turn. Every card was unsuited and finally the river card .... 2.

"Gre-e-eat! I laughed, as I scooped up the chips which now made me chip leader, "Yea-ah!"

"You Jammy river rat you're now't else," joked Daz followed by "Well done Tas ... good luck!" as he handed me the bounty money.

"Thanks Daz!" I said as I put the money into my wallet.

Two deals later and I was the dealer. My two holding cards were pocket eights and both my opponents went all in. My mind flashed back to Tasmania where I had pocket eights and finished up with Quads. Also it flashed through my mind that pocket eights had somehow always treated me kindly and that's what decided me.

"Yeah alright .... I call!"

All cards on the table and one player had A/Q and the other had A/J.

"U-um," I thought, a J - Q or an Ace and I'm gone.

Nevertheless, on the flop I was pleased to see - 2/7/8 all off suit.

"Great!" I mused, "Neither of 'em can hit a flush or a straight and I've got a set."

The turn card put me out of my misery because it was another 7 giving me a full house. My nephew James and Luggy were watching and both congratulated me, as did Daz and my opponents.

"Well that's one bloody good night you've had John," laughed Luggy. You're goin' home tonight with a bit o' change in your pocket."

"I'm proud of you Uncle John," said James giving me a hug, "wait till I tell mi' mam tonight ... she won't half be pleased!" He must have forgot he was allowed to call me Tas. Other players congratulated me as well because two weeks previously on my special birthday, I had left money behind the bar for each player to have a drink. "Cheers John ... you deserve it!" they all reiterated!

On the way home I was well pleased with the outcome but, by now, I realised that my next game would be another game entirely.

Something happened just recently that I found rather funny and once again it involved Daz. "He'd roughly about 50000 chips and I had about 40000. The blinds were sky high and I was in danger of being blinded out. My holding cards were K/J suited and Darren went all in. All the other players folded and it came round to me. I pondered a little and decided it was worth the risk and I called him.

"Oh not you again Tas ... I've got a funny feeling about this."

On turning the card he had pocket Queens. The flop was 7/8/10 and the turn was .... 2. I was ready for shaking hands but then the river card was a ....K!

I was obviously pleased with the outcome but then came the funny part. Daz threw his chips over to me saying, "You jammy git .... put that in your fucking book!"

That was funny but, to enhance the laughter, a couple of hands later he took a stack of chips of Procky. Turning to me with a grin on his face he said, I'm just stacking 'em up and getting them ready for you Tas."

I had to laugh but it didn't happen. A couple of hands later I went All In with A/K and was called with Q/9. I didn't hit anything and a nine turned up on the river. That's poker!

Talk about uncanny things that happen in poker, something unbelievable happened to Steve. Being an avid poker player, he'd played the game for many years and knew all the ups and downs of the game ... or so he thought. As it happened a few of the lads took themselves off to Las Vegas every year to try out their luck amongst the big boys in the casinos during the World Series. It was costly but they likened it to a mini holiday. Well, Steve told me he'd always wanted to do it and he enlightened me about following his dream.

"Just listen to this John ... you'll never believe what happened to me when I went to Vegas in 2013 to qualify for the World Series.

"Did you go along with some of the lads? I asked.

"No, I went at the same time, but I went there with my wife Sue."

"Oh, does your wife like poker as well Steve?"

"No, she went simply to relax and enjoy the sights and also to give me a bit of support. What happened was that my daughter Kelly, who is a keen poker player in her own right, wanted to treat me and her mum. She bought us two plane tickets and booked me and Sue into the Rio Hotel."

"E-eh, that was nice of her. But then it would have cost you a bomb to enter World Series wouldn't it Steve?"

"Aye, you're right there but there was satellite program which organised a small event. For an entrance fee of 380 dollars the event gave competitors the chance to qualify for the main contest. I'd always dreamed of playing in the World Series and I thought ... what the 'eck, this is my big chance."

"Oh great Steve, how did you fair ... did you win a bundle?"

"Ha, ha! he laughed. "You'll not believe this John, but I was knocked out of the competition on my very first hand."

"Give over ... you're kidding me!"

"No ... so help me God, as I live and breathe ... that's the Gospel truth."

"OK. I believe you but tell me ... what happened?"

"Well, the very first two cards I picked up were A/Q and, believe it or not, the flop was A/Q/J all unsuited. What do you think of that?"

"Wow two top pair on the flop and chance of a full house ... that's a great hand in anybody's book. So ... what happened?"

"What happened? Well, I readily bet 5000 chips and a bloke called me and another one went all in."

"Oh 'eck ... did he have a pocket pair?

"No he didn't ... that's what I was thinking, but I took the risk anyway and called him."

"If he didn't have a pocket pair ... what did he have?"

"Believe it or not he had J/9 and he hit a10 on the turn and a K on the river to give him a straight."

"Arr-gh, that was unlucky, but then again ... that's poker."

"Yeah, you're right there ... and didn't I know it!"

"I bet you were gutted."

"You can say that again. The first thing I did was to go to the bathing pool where Sue was relaxing. I got out my camera and held up my entrance ticket to the World Series and asked Sue to take my photo. And after that I went and dived in the pool to cool off."

"Never mind Steve you can always say you came first in the World Series. Ha ha ... first out!"

****

In two years of playing the game Poker I have only seen a Royal Flush once, and it happened to be Steve at one of Daz's events. The pot was over £700 and he decided to donate it all to the charity he was running ... what a good fella!

CHAPTER 3 - ANDY

Texas Hold'em was always held on a Thursday evening at Ighten Leigh Club and, as each player gradually got knocked out of the competition, a cash table was set up. Personally I love the game of Texas hold'em but playing poker for money is a different ball game ... it is not for me as I consider it dangerous. In a knockout event you can only lose your stake money after playing for an hour or so whereas a player can easily lose a lot of money in a single hand on a cash table. A fine example that springs to mind is when two regular players, Gordon and Lee got knocked out of the competition and they both joined others on a cash table.

There were eight players and after an hour or so it was relatively even. Then one hand, Gordon's holding cards were 5/5. Lee was the first person in line and he bet £20 and another player called. All the other players folded around to Gordon and he called. To Gordon's delight the flop was K/5/5.

"Great!" he thought, " I hope someone's got a king."

Lee was first to act and he raised the bet to £40. The other player folded so it was heads up - Gordon against Lee. Gordon paused for a while and then flat called.

The turn card was an 8 and this time Lee raised it to £80.

As it happened, Lee had twenty minutes earlier stung Gordon with a set of 5's. Gordon purposely studied the table cards and, hoping to throw Lee off the scent, he asked, "For God's sake Lee ... you haven't got a set of fives again have you?"

"Ha ha! laughed Lee, "I've got better than that. Anyway ... that's for me to know and you to find out."

"Righto." said Gordon with a serious face, I believe you ... I raise it to £160."

"Wow!" yelped Lee, and he immediately raised it a further £60 and called All In.

Gordon called and Lee happily turned over K/K with a big beaming smile on his face... he'd actually hit a full house on the flop. But the smile quickly turned to a pout when Gordon laid down his pocket 5's.

"Arr-rg-gh! groaned Lee," I don't believe it ... I feel as though I've just been mugged."

This incident is the very reason why I try to avoid cash tables.

****

Steve and I tried hard to get willing folk to be characters in our new story. Most of them were unwilling to bare their souls and I could understand why. Nevertheless, others were keen on the idea. Two willing participants were Andrew Hennessey and Andrew Holt.

The first one to call me was Andy Holt. I was soon to learn that he is a very down to earth man but his business acumen is second to none.

"Hello John, Andy Holt here, Steve Wood told me about your new venture and I'm willing to put my head on the chopping block. ... I think it could make good reading."

"Oh that's great Andy ... how do you want to go about it?"

"Well I'm extremely busy at the moment but I'll tell you what ... can you give me a ring at 11o'clock tomorrow morning and I'll let you know then if I can fit you in."

"Superb Andy ..... cheers!"

I did ring him next day and he asked me to come down to his factory the following day at 3-30pm.

He gave me directions to an industrial estate at Altham, near Padiham. It was easy to find as, on entering the compound, it was the second building on the right and had a great big sign containing the four letters, 'WHAM'. He later told me he had conjured the name from the fact that his firm was 'WHAT MORE UK, and he took the first three letters of 'WHAT and the first letter of MORE.

On entering the building his receptionist guided me to his office on the second floor.

"Hiya John," he greeted me, "come in and make yourself comfortable. But first things first would you like a brew?"

"Yes please Andy ... thank you very much." The office was rather big and luxurious but Andy's friendliness put me completely at ease.

"Right where do I start?" he said in a laid back attitude. "I was born on Patten Street, in the Trafalgar area of Burnley where I believe you lived as a child John."

"That's right Andy. In fact, I lived on Albion Street for the first twenty years of my life and our back bedroom overlooked the roof tops of Patten Street."

"Twenty years eh. Well I didn't live there very long as all the terraced houses were due to be demolished to make way for Trafalgar Flats. I was just a few month's old when my mum and dad moved into a council house on Stoops Estate."

"Oh so you won't really recall Trafalgar days then?"

"That's right but I certainly well remember living in poverty in that cold damp scheme house, but it was nothing compared to how my parents and grandparents lived. One winter it was absolutely freezing and they'd ran out of coal. In order to ward off the cold and keep warm, my grandad ripped off all the skirting boards throughout the house and chopped up a couple of chairs."

"Oh 'eck Andy ... I'll bet the council weren't very pleased."

"You can say that again ... but it was a case of break the law and keep warm or abide by it and freeze to death."

"Ha ha, you're right there. It puts me in mind of when we used to pick coal off the railway lines. People knew they were breaking the law, but they used the same expression that you have just used. Anyway how did you cope with the conditions?"

"Well I didn't know anything else and the way I saw it was that everyone of the neighbours were in the same boat as we were. I was always a little laid back and I just took everything in my stride as though it was normal."

"It very much reminds me of my childhood days."

"Yeah, I can well imagine. Anyway, as I grew bigger I became very enterprising and engaged in many ways of making brass. I'd knock on doors around the estate and buy half decent shirts, coats and other clothing at a rock bottom price and then I'd go to a jumble sale and sell them at four times what I'd paid for them. Mind you, they were still getting a bargain. Besides the jumble sales I also had regular customers for working shirts and trousers. Another thing I did was to scavenge items from skips and flog them on. However, I soon discovered that it was hard to find anything worth while in Burnley skips. So I took myself off to Whalley where the people appeared more affluent. I picked up many discarded bicycles and did them up. I used to strip them down and use the spare parts off one bike to repair another. I then cleaned them up and painted them. Though I say it myself they looked pretty good and I easily sold them."

"Nice Andy, nice ... I like it! So I take it you were never short of cash?"

"John, I can honestly say that at times I had more money in my pocket than my dad who had been working hard all week. And the job he did was not an easy one. I was told that my grandad worked at Moorhouse Brewery as a lorry driver but, as he was only small, another one of his jobs was to clean out the beer kegs. He could crawl into a beer barrel and the job was to clean them thoroughly with a scrubbing brush using chemicals. Fumes from the kegs used to irritate his eyes and he eventually went blind. I'm not saying that the fumes caused it but they didn't help."

"E-eh that's sad that is."

"Yeah, it was very sad indeed.

"What school did you go to Andy when you left the juniors?"

"Well I did well in my eleven plus exams and I went to Burnley Grammar School."

"Did you find it hard work there?"

"No it came quite natural to me. In fact there were times when I was quite disruptive ... but, then again, that's my nature. If I didn't accept something I would try to change it."

"Did it work?"

"No, not really but I did it all the same."

"How did you fare overall there?"

"Actually I was doing very well and, when I reached the age of fifteen, I decided to stay on for a higher education."

"Oh, did you go on to university then?

"No. That was my intention but then when I was just turned sixteen my father died. I was completely and utterly devastated. He was only 38 and he had a massive brain haemorrhage. This was a major turning point in my life."

"Oh, I sorry about that ... I know how you must have felt because my dad died at the age of 52 and I was devastated."

"Yeah life can be a swine can't it? Anyway from that point on I changed my lifestyle. I pondered for a while in limbo and then decided to go to Nelson College to train as a tool maker. After a year I got a job in a tool making factory and really enjoyed it. The job came so natural to me and I won a 'Tool Maker Of The Year' award. By the time I was twenty I was put in charge of the firm and by the age of twenty-two I was running the place. I stayed there a while but I always yearned to set up on my own. Over the years I gleaned as much experience as I could and then in November 1999 I moved into this building and I've been here ever since."

"Did you not think you were taking a risk Andy?"

"John, the way I look at life, sometimes you've got to take the bull by its horns and that's exactly what I did. Besides I wanted to create my own designs and special engineering tools."

"You must have a gift Andy ... that's all I can say."

"Aye!" he laughed heartily, "Maybe."

"It's all interesting stuff Andy, but just one more thing before we get talking about poker. How did you come to own Accrington Stanley Football Club?"

"O-oh that's another story and it can be a pain in the arse. I never wanted to own a football club but I made the fatal mistake of going to a match with some of the lads and meeting people involved with the club. They were a good crowd and the club was on its last legs and struggling to pay the wages. I was encouraged to go along to a meeting with a solicitor and a bank manager. To be fair I was advised not to touch it with a large barge pole. But then what I did, so as to help them out, I promised I would pay their wages for two months and if I decided against buying the club they could keep the money as a token gift."

"That was good of you."

"Aye may be it was but, to cut a long story short, I did sign a contract and now it's mine and I'm stuck with it!"

"Stuck with it ... that sounds a bit gloomy."

"Don't get me wrong. What it is ... after I've been working here all week I sometimes feel like a break. But, as I own the club, I have to attend every match and go to board meetings afterwards. It can be rather stressful but, the way I look at it, it's good for the community and that gives me a good feeling."

"Aye, I imagine it does. I believe that Accrington Stanley football Club also owned the Crown Pub in Accrington."

"That's right it was part of the deal but, before I signed a contact, I dealt with the greedy lease owners. The pub was on lease and every time it made a decent profit the voracious owners demanded more rent. Consequently the pub was cast afloat in the ocean without a paddle. The lease was coming to an end and so I stepped in and bought it."

"Good on you. Anyroad, I believe in your teens you and Luggy lived on the same estate and you were best friends."

"You're right there, we were inseparable and, like other teenagers, we got up to loads of antics. Luggy was a great friend even though he was mental. I couldn't complain because so was I. I've got to admit he was a good sportsman and he revelled in whatever sport he played. One time we went fishing for trout at Lothersdale and he was a fine fisherman too. We hired a boat but I couldn't be arsed with setting up the rod and I asked Luggy to just put a hook on the end of the line for me. He was fishing from the port side of the boat and I was fishing from the starboard side. It was a private lake and the rules were to use fly fishing tactics only. Unbeknown to Luggy, I was using bread. Within minutes of throwing in my line I had a seven pounder on the end of it. 'You lucky bastard,' he called me but, within minutes, I had another on the line. This mode of events carried on and after a couple of hours I'd caught many more fish than he had. We threw lots of them back into the lake and, because we had to pay for our catch according to weight, we hid a couple of big ones underneath a car mat in the boot of the car. When Luggy found out I had been using bread he nearly kicked me out of the boat. No more to be said ... you can imagine the names he called me."

"Ha ha, I can that!"

"Ever since then I constantly remind him that I am the better fisherman to which he always replies with a grin on his face ... 'You cheeky cheating bastard!'"

"Oh, that seems a bit mild for Luggy."

"Yeah, I suppose it is ... he doesn't mince about with words."

"You're not kidding! Was he the same as a lad?"

"He was that ... he hasn't changed one ha'peth. Like I mentioned earlier ... we were both mental. On saying that, Luggy and I have only ever fell out twice and we were back friends five minutes later."

"Oh this should be interesting."

"The first time was when I was doing a job at my sister's house and Luggy offered to help me. I was rewiring her house and the ceiling needed repairing. The old ceiling needed dropping and replacing with plasterboards. What a dirty job that was ... it was constructed of thin wooden lats and old plaster. We were covered in shit from head to toe and the fine plaster got into our eyes and other crevices."

"I know exactly what you mean ... I've dropped a few old ceilings myself in my time."

"Anyway, for a breath of fresh air we decided to eat outside in the garden. We were both hungry so I went to the shop and bought two potato pies and two meat pies. I left them with Luggy and went inside to make a brew. When I came outside I couldn't believe it ... he'd scoffed three pies and left me with a meat and potato pie."

"Ha ha, I'll bet you were pleased."

"Oh yeah, I was pleased all right. 'Where the fuck is my meat pie you greedy bastard.' I bawled. He just sat there smiling like a Cheshire cat. I did no more ... I picked up a piece of wood and I chased him down the street shouting, 'I'll knock your fucking head off!' He still kept laughing but I gradually caught up with him and whacked him on his back with the plank. We had a few words but later on we went for a pint together."

"I like it. And now what about the second incidence?"

"Well what it is ... Luggy was a big chap and weighed over twenty stone. Not only was he big, he was nimble too and could readily handle himself. The trouble was that if he got into an argument with anyone he would never back down and constantly ended up using his fist. He had a terrific punch and when he hit someone they knew they'd been hit. Because of his reputation, just like in a western film, some nutters would taunt him, inciting him to fight. It was like a red flag to a bull and he'd just set into them and lay them out. I knew he could handle himself but, on occasions, I would often encourage him to let it go. After one scenario like this we got arguing amongst ourselves. I can't remember what the argument was about, but we were stood face to face and he attempted to whack me. To avoid the blow I leant backwards but, unluckily for me, he struck me in the throat. I immediately thought, 'Fucking hell ... I don't want any more of this!' He could see he'd hurt me and was full of remorse. We shook hands and carried on being best buddies."

"That's good to hear ... I'm proud of you both!"

"Later, during my business life I lost touch with Luggy due to a personal injury where I sustained serious injury to my chest, my left arm and my left leg. I was in hospital for a while and on morphine for five years to combat the pain. The injury left me in a wheelchair for a while but, lucky for me, friends like Luggy and Johnny Mac, would come and wheel me about. I appreciated what they were doing but, feeling way down low, I just couldn't laugh and joke with them. Business wise I felt out of the game but luckily I had good staff to run my business affairs. Because of the incident I lost touch with many of my mates. I felt way down in the dumps but then, my resilience started to kick in. To get back up onto my horse and feel normal again, I decided to go to Read Club and that's where my poker life began."

"So you met up with some old friends again I take it?"

"Yeah and one of them was Luggy. However the Luggy after my accident wasn't the same Luggy as before it. He'd recently had a mild stroke and was limping around. Likewise I wasn't the same person as before. Hence the good old days were behind us and gone forever. Where did we go from there? We talked and laughed about our past lives and actually found it amusing that we had gone from doing things to talking about things."

"Well, one thing's for sure ... Luggy can certainly do that."

"Ha ha, he can that. Anyway John, that's enough of my business and social life. How about another brew and then we can talk about poker?"

After a short break he started chatting again and this time it was about the extraordinary game.

"John," he stressed, "I've never been one for fancy cars and going to posh places. Although on saying that I do need a luxurious one for running my business. A rich couple think nothing of having a meal and a bottle of wine and not getting any change from a thousand pounds. They love to be seen in this kind of environment ... it's good for their ego. But, to me, it's not the real world. Poker is important to me because it puts me back amongst the lads where we can all socialise together on even ground. If you go to a fancy place you might talk to one or two of the so called elite people but you don't really know them. But when I'm sat around a poker table, that's when I feel at home. It breaks down barriers. I like the way that you shake hands and exchange names with a newcomer. I can honestly say that it puts me at ease and releases a lot of stress. There's lots of f-ffing and blinding going on but it's all in good humour ... I love it. It's great when someone calls me a river rat, a lucky jammy bastard or other chosen names. It truly relaxes me on a Friday night after a week of hassling and dealing with wealthy clients."

"Have you been playing the game long Andy?"

"No, not like some of them. I've been playing it about five years, but like I said it really relaxes me. I remember when I first started playing at Read Club. All the lads encouraged me but I was constantly losing all my chips and forever having to re-buy.

"Yeah I know the feeling ... that was me two years ago in Tasmania."

Andy started laughing, "Yeah but then I got the hang of it and, one particular month, I won it four times on the trot ... it was like taking candy from a baby ha, ha!"

"I bet you enjoyed that ... it's a good feeling when things are going your way isn't it? Anyway ... do you ever bluff?

"It depends on how I feel. As the night goes on and I've had a few pints the more I bluff. In fact, one time when I'd had a few bevvies before going to the club I was well pie-eyed by nine o'clock and, after the break, I was going All In with really crap hands and winning."

"Aye, it's a funny game isn't it? Anyway, can you remember any particular hands that stands out in your mind?"

"Oh aye ... I once had a Royal Flush', and it stands out alright because every one of the bastards folded."

"Never mind ... you'd still have won what was in the pot for a Royal Flush?"

"Yeah, it was £121, but the club was packed that night and after I'd paid for a round of drinks for everyone I finished up having to put £10 towards it."

"Ha, ha ... thanks Andy ... just one more question. How do you play pocket aces?"

"Well, all I can say about that is that at the end of the day it is just a pair, and one pair rarely wins a hand. So what I do depends on what position I am in on the table. If I am first to play I put a lot a chips in the pot to frighten some players off. But if I'm in a late position and others have made a large bid ... I just call."

"U-um, I think I'm going to have to play like that because by hanging back with pocket aces I've been stung loads of times."

"Yeah, haven't we all? I actually prefer A/K suited to pocket aces."

"Yeah ... I like that hand as well."

"Another hand that sticks in my memory is when I got pocket sevens and the flop was 5/6/7 all clubs. The turn card was another 7, and the river was 8 of clubs. There was a fair pot a so I pushed All In with my quad sevens and, to my surprise, a player called me."

"Great ... you'd be well pleased?"

"Yeah, I was that until he turned his cards and the swine had a straight flush. I was gutted ... and even more so because he only held one of the calling cards in his hand."

"I'll bet you came out with a few choice words."

"Did I! Talk about you jammy river rat ... that was mild to what I called him. Joking aside I still go on about that hand every time I play poker at Read"

"Good, I'll listen out for it the next time you're there."

"Ha ha ... you do that!"

"Cheers Andy!" I said shaking his hand, "And thanks for having me."

"You're welcome John ... if you're ever passing call in for a brew."

That was the end of our conversation ... all light-hearted stuff and I've got to admit I thoroughly enjoyed it. Before leaving he gave me four patterned tea mugs representing Accrington Stanley Football Club. Each one had a design of Accrington's Coat of Arms. I gave one to my son, one to my brother and one to Steve. A large stone carved shield depicting Accrington's Coat of Arms can be seen in the Accrington Market Hall on the balcony close to the upstairs cafe.

Since I starting writing this book the Corona Virus pandemic put the brakes on things all over the country. It came to my knowledge that Andy's firm WHATMORE, made and supplied lots of masks and plastic face covers for the NHS at cost price. It struck me that he was once more thinking about the community.

PHOTOGRAPHS - THE POKER WORLD

Andy at work

Sean

Irish John

Mark, Andy and Gordon in deep thought

Procky

Billy

129

Steve in Las Vegas

Darren

A young Steve

Big Pete, Billy... Colette at the bar

Rishton Rick

James

Rebecca

Tim

Pete in charge at Read

Darren in charge

Andy

Rebecca taking orders

Tas - first win in Tasmania

Roger - chip leader

Lee

Elliot

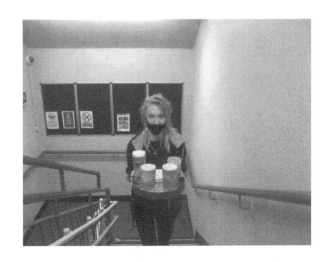

Rebecca - hard working girl

Tas - second win in Tasmania

Woody

James

All-in Andy

Brian

Looks like Lionel has just scooped Billy

Nicola

Cash game - Luggy and Andrew

Thinking about it

Luggy and Steve

Lee and James

Sunny's family

Steve, John and Sunny

Roger and Gordon - four of a kind

Let's have a break

Tim

You're bluffing!

Colette - should I go for it or what?

Steve

Big Comp

Procky and Baron

Vicky - winner of The Joker's wild Comp. WOW... £3000!

John and Vicky at Goliath

Joker's Wild

John, Tas and Vicky at Goliath

Louis

Mates, Danny and Ian

Darren and Gale

Peter

Karen

Brian

Colette

Vicky competing in Joker's Wild

Tas and John at Goliath

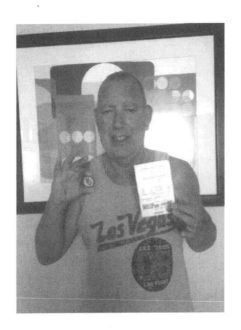

Steve - First Out medal at World Series

Phil

Tas

Lionel

157

James - Christmas trophy

Another win for Vicky

John and Vicky enjoying the night

John, Lionel and Vicky - yet another win

Gary

All the players in the final game

Stop thinking and just call!

Waiting for the big game to begin

Andy in deep thought

Luggy, Irish John and Daz

Vicky and Elsina

Elsina

163

James, Andrew and Roger

Andy - finished third in the comp

Steve with runner's up medal

Andrew on left was very lucky to win the comp. Steve
didn't want the publicity of being champion ......ha ha!

CHAPTER 4 - LUGGY

Sitting around a poker table, Luggy is a character on his own and he loves chatting about his young life when he was fit and strong, and openly boasts that he could handle himself ... when he hit somebody they stayed down.

Whilst playing poker, no matter who is sat on his table, f-ffing and blinding are part of his vocabulary. Another mannerism is that he can fart for England. He often laughs and brags that he can fart at will. If Steve happens to be sat on his table he uses a deodorant to combat the smell, but it doesn't put Luggy off and, even if there are ladies sat at the table, his antics never change. In his own words he has no favourites.

"What's up with you" he openly laughs, "we all have to do it?"

"Yeah ... but not every other minute," one of the lads would comment whilst others cracked up laughing.

On saying that, of all the people I have come across I have never met a funnier bloke than Luggy. Despite being boisterous some of his tales are quite humorous and entertaining. Whilst sat at the poker he often relates many tales of his younger life and one story he told was really funny albeit quite tragic. For some reason we were chatting about false teeth and how some people come to lose their natural teeth.

"E-eh, I haven't had any teeth since I was fourteen years old," he said with a cheeky toothless grin."

"Fourteen?" I queried, "That's a bit young," what happened?"

"Well I was always into making a bob or two whenever I got the chance and one job I did was to trim the lawn of an elderly lady. It was a large grassy area and as I was going backward and forward with the mower I ran over the electric cable and cut it. I didn't have a Stanley knife on me so I asked the lady if she had a sharp knife. I carefully cut through the outer sheath and then attempted to strip the inner small wires with my teeth."

"Oh don't tell me you hadn't switched off the electric?"

"You've got it in one John!"

"Blimey, was there one big bang?"

"Well, I can imagine there was but I don't really know. The next thing I remember was waking up in hospital three days later and ... I'd lost all my teeth!"

"I had to laugh again because like I said ... it was tragic albeit very funny."

Luggy didn't mind me laughing as he thought it was an amusing tale too and he would tell it on a regular basis.

I asked Luggy if he would like to be a character in the book and he was very keen.

"Yeah Tas, I'd loved to ... why don't you come around to my house tomorrow and we'll talk about it."

"Great Luggy ... I'll be there."

He lived at 34 Fenwick Street in the Bleak House area of town and I reached there about three o'clock to find Luggy sat in an arm chair with a plaster cast on his left foot. He'd just recently come out of hospital after having two toes removed due to infection caused by diabetes. Despite his setback he was in a very jovial mood. He'd just been to Burnley General Hospital for a check up and to have a drain removed. He'd driven there and parked on St Cuthbert's Street near to the hospital gates. On crossing Briercliffe Road he lost his footing and fell into the gutter. He couldn't believe how many cars just drove past him. Then a young lady, who had a child on the back seat of her car, pulled over and, after helping him to his feet, she gave him a lift to the hospital reception. He offered her some money but she refused to take it.

"She was an angel in disguise," he laughed. "Anyroad, first things first, ... let's put the kettle on."

"Yeah thanks Luggy ... it sounds good to me."

After the brew he started to narrate some interesting tales. We got so engrossed that it was seven o'clock before I left. After telling me the hospital episode he recited a few of his antics.

"I was born on 4th of December 1966, and at six week's old I came to live in this house and, but for a few months, I have lived here ever since. After meeting my partner Tracey, we moved into a house on Belmont Street, Brunshaw. But shortly after, my parents moved out of this house and so I moved back in. This is a good house and the rent was £10 a week cheaper which was a lot of money back then."

"So you spent all your childhood years here Luggy?"

"I did that and one of my first recollections is of my parents splitting up. I don't know the reason why, but I do know that my mother went living down south in Weston Super Mare leaving my dad to bring up me and my elder brother, Craig. Dad found it a hard task being a single parent and had to work various jobs, including shift work. Luckily for me, Craig helped Dad best he could and he was my protector. Up to the age of thirteen, my grandparents lived on Elgin Crescent and I spent lots of time there. I never missed calling at their house after school but sadly, they both passed away whilst I was still very young."

"O-oh, what a shame ... I can imagine that hit you hard Luggy."

"It did John but I still had my older brother to count on. It seemed strange not being able to visit them in that little house as I passed it on my way home from school. But sometime later James Clancey's' brother Dale, moved in there and, as I knew him, it made me feel better."

"I was a keen sportsman and my brother Craig encouraged me all the way. I was a good footballer and enjoyed playing 11-a-side as a centre midfielder. I regularly played five-a-side and a memorable occasion was when our team won the five-a-side league. I remember scoring the winning goal to clinch the title ... and what a scorcher it was. From just within my own half I sent it screaming into the top corner of the small net giving the goalkeeper no chance. I was certainly the hero of the day ... my mates went wild. But, even though I enjoyed playing football, my favourite game was cricket and I was good at it.   At the age of thirteen I attended Ivy Bank School and was selected to play for Lancashire and played at Old Trafford against Yorkshire. I was a medium pace spin bowler and I took three wickets and scored twenty eight runs at number three bat. Sadly I only played one game as my dad couldn't afford the expense needed to travel around the country with the team. At the time I didn't understand the value of money or the lack of it. Hence, I felt out of joint and let down."

"A-ah, what a shame. Anyway, I bet you were popular at school."

"Ha ha," he laughed, "it was just the opposite. I was forever in trouble and I got expelled for hitting the games' teacher. He came out with some words to me that I will never forget. 'Ludlam, you are the finest schoolboy cricketer I have ever come across but, as a scholar, you are a complete arsehole!' I had to go in front of the Board of Governors and I got expelled. From there I went to Padiham Adult Centre known locally as the ultimate school for bad lads and lasses."

"Oh 'eck ... I'll bet you didn't like it there then?"

"You're wrong John ... in fact, it was good for me as we only had a one hour lesson in the morning and the rest of the day was for games. Also, one day a week, I was allowed to go on a work experience at Hill's Pop and this introduced me to the big wide world."

"And did you go working there when you left school?"

"No, at the age of sixteen I went working as a glass cutter for a double glazing firm. I enjoyed the job and worked there for about twelve years and then decided I wanted to work for myself. By now my partner Tracey and I had two boys, Sam and Gary. They meant the world to me and I was determined to work my guts out in order to support them. But it wasn't all work and no play. Together with Tracey and my two boys we spent a lot of time in Cornwall. I had a caravan on 'White Acres,' a caravan site set amongst glorious countryside. It was close to a forest hideaway where roe deer, birds and other types of wildlife thrived. Whilst I was there I forgot about life's pressures and I was totally relaxed. I loved to do a spot of fishing and became known amongst the locals as 'Uncle Luggy.' At home, in my spare time I loved to go rabbitting with my dog. Not far from my house is a large expanse of open moorland leading to the foothills of Hameldon Hill. It was known as the 'Clough' and I loved nothing more than foraging the open grassland with my faithful hound. Also close to the foothills was a gully filled with water from the surrounding hills. It was known locally as 'The Sheep Dip' and was an ideal place for swimming."

"I know the place well Luggy ... I used to go swimming in it myself."

"Anyway, back to the way I made my living. Over the years I did all kinds of work, bobbing and weaving in and out of different professions. I became a market trader selling my wares up and down the country. I definitely felt I had found my niche and during the following fifteen years I travelled to markets in Catterick, Penrith, Uttoxeter,

Beeston and other outlying places and I loved every minute of it. I worked all the hours that God sent, working wherever destiny sent me but I always spent Sundays on Catterick Market. The market trade was good to me and I made a good living from it. It was so good that I set up a Flower Company. I did this as a front so I could hide some collateral made from cash-in-hand deals."

"So you liked to keep a few irons in the fire then Luggy?"

"Too bloody true ... I'd tackle anything to earn a crust. In between time I worked for Andy Holt who'd been my friend from childhood days and was his right hand man. I enjoyed working for Andy, driving him all over the country to different functions and venues. One time he was going abroad on a business trip for ten days and asked me to drive him to Manchester Airport. He'd just bought a brand new Jaguar XK8 and it was a beauty. When I dropped him off he just put the keys in my hand and told me to enjoy myself whilst he was away. It was great!"

"I believe you and Andy were childhood friends."

"That's right ... as youths we were as thick as thieves and were forever getting up to mischief. One time we went to a Chinese restaurant and when it came to pay the bill Andy went to the toilet. After about twenty minutes I realised that he must have legged it as the toilets were near to some exit stairs. So likewise, I did the same and, when I got outside, Andy was in a taxi waiting for me and laughing his head off. "Get in quick," he laughed, let's get out of here!"

"Ha ha I think that's something we've all done at one time or another."

"Yeah I'm sure we have. Anyway, another thing about Andy is that he is very competitive. It doesn't matter whether it's business or pleasure ... he doesn't like to lose. One good example is playing darts. I was always a decent dart player and we used to play for a pound. We played lots of games but he hardly won any. One day in the Gretna Pub, after I'd thrashed him a few times, he was furious and asked for a handicap. So I agreed to stand on a buffet which meant I was throwing downhill. I'd just two darts in my hand and I needed the bull. I took aim and lobbed the dart. Unbelievingly it landed smack in the bulls-eye ... I couldn't believe it."

"Ha ha ... I'll bet Andy wasn't pleased."

"You're right there. The next thing I know he called me a jammy bastard and then kicked the stool over that I was standing on. I went crashing to the floor, still with a dart in my hand, and fell badly onto my left arm. In a reaction I threw the remaining dart and, God's truth, it also landed in the bull."

"Ha ha, how was your arm?"

"Well it turned out I'd two hairline fractures near to my elbow. At first Andy called me a soft bastard and told me to stop whinging. However, to give him his due, when he realised I was hurt he called for his wife to take me to hospital. I gave him some stick the following day when I arrived at work with my arm in a sling."

"I take it you were still buddies?

"Oh aye, course we were ... we never ever fell out for long. Anyway, a few years later he went living in Huddersfield and worked for a firm called British Bungs. It was known locally as 'The Bung Factory'. They supplied plastic bungs to big breweries throughout the country."

"Excuse me for being thick but what is a bung?"

"Well, it is a plastic device that pub landlords used to replace corks in the top of a beer barrel. Before a barrel can be used it has to be tapped and vented to allow the beer to flow. That's where Andy came into his own ... he was very clever at inventing different devices."

"Did you lose track of him when he went living in Huddersfield?"

"No. In fact, I used to go over there regularly on a Honda 750cc motorbike. One funny tale is when I won a massive teddy bear in a raffle. Andy's wife had just had a little girl and I thought it would be a nice present. So I decided to ride over there with the teddy bear strapped to my back. It must have looked hilarious as I passed many cars on the motorway."

"Yeah ... I'll bet it did. Anyroad, how long did he live in Huddersfield?"

"U-um not all that long. I think he was a little unsettled and he decided to come back to Burnley. That's when he set up his 'WHAM' enterprise in Altham."

"I believe you worked for him now and again."

"Yeah I did and it was great. Like you know, Andy is one of the boys when he is playing poker. But being in big business he often has to mix with the elite and attend conferences and other affairs. When he goes to these meetings he has to dress up in his best bib and tucker ... collar and tie and all that Jazz. Believe it or not he hired a suit for me and took me with him on a couple of occasions. But he made sure I was on my best behaviour."

"Ha ha!" I laughed, I'll bet he did ... I can imagine that wasn't very easy. How did you fit in?"

"Well believe it or not John I had a great time. The first event he took me to was held at the Grosvenor Hotel in London and we were sat on the same table as David Jason and Frank Bruno. The second venue was at a sportsman's dinner in Rotherham. Michael Parkinson was there as were Bobby Knut, Peter Elliot and Trevor Cherry."

"I'll bet you enjoyed the meals Luggy."

"I did but do you know something ... on the way home, both Andy and I said we'd have much preferred a dish of pie and mushy peas."

Once again I had to laugh.

****

During our conversation I heard a parrot squawking in another room which got Luggy talking about one of his hobbies.

"Eh John, I've got a big back garden and for years I've bred birds. I built three 8ft x 4ft sheds and each had a long flight area attached to it. I had Rose ring neck parakeets, Cockatiels, Golden Mantels, Red-rumps, Rosella and Prince of Wales parrots. They bred like rabbits and at one time I had over seventy birds in the aviary. I also had some Chinese Quail ... they looked like tennis balls on legs. They gave me a lot of pleasure. I loved sitting in the garden listening to them make music and my next door neighbour enjoyed them too. Another hobby of mine was fishing and every week I bought the Angling Times. Whilst the wife was hoovering the carpets and doing the housework I'd spend a couple of hours in one of the aviaries and sit there reading the magazine. The birds would be twittering away and I used to get covered in bird shit but I didn't mind ... I loved it. At the time I was working the markets and I always had a large Iveco van parked outside my house. This went on for years and then a new neighbour moved in next door and he was a nasty piece of work. He complained bitterly about the van and also the birds. I wouldn't care but he had a great massive fir tree in his front garden which cast a dark shadow over my house. When I refused to move the van we had a few cross words and he mumbled under his breath that something might happen to my van. I warned him that if anything happened I'd know where to come and I threatened to banjo him."

"And did anything untoward happen to the van Luggy?"

"No but something else did. I took my wife and kids for a week's holiday in Cornwall. I always made sure when I went away that my birds were well looked after and I used to leave a key with a lady neighbour. When I got back I collected the key and asked if everything was alright. She shook her head and I knew instantly that something was afoot. I couldn't believe it when she told me that every single bird was dead."

"Blimey Luggy ... was it your next door neighbour?"

"Well John, I'll never know ... I couldn't prove a thing."

"Does he still live there?" I asked rather intrigued.

"Yeah he does and we just barely put up with each other. Anyway John, just look outside ... the fir tree's still there."

Sure enough, there it stood and it was absolutely gigantic.

"Did you breed any more birds after that episode?"

"No, did I 'eck as like. Due to ill health I couldn't be bothered to start up afresh. In fact I tended to neglect the garden and it became like a jungle. The funny thing is that an unusual tropical type plant started to grow and it's now massive. I didn't plant it ... all I can think is it must have come about due to all the bird droppings."

"Aye you're probably right there Luggy"

After another brew I broached him on another topic. "Right, I've heard you mention that you were the landlord of a pub at one time."

"Yeah, that's right. After fifteen years working the markets I ventured into the pub trade and took on the Alma Pub on Accrington Road. It was a good old fashioned drinking pub frequented by many of the locals. Some of the customers were tough, hard working men who enjoyed a pint of bitter after a hard day's slog. Others could be rough and rowdy. But I sorted things out and they soon realised I wasn't a man to be messed about with. I have had a lot of fights in my time but I have never been beaten. I was a good, big 'un. In the same breath I have never hit anyone for nothing. After just a few weeks the pub was running smoothly and I had a good clientele. Every Saturday afternoon and Wednesday evening we had a good session of Texas Hold'em Poker for a few quid and everybody had a good laugh and thoroughly enjoyed it. Most of the pubs in Burnley didn't open their doors until 3 o'clock in the afternoon but I always opened up at 11 o'clock in the morning. Believe it or not I took more money in the first few hours than other pubs were taking all day. By gum John ... they were good times."

"Did you ever have any incidents involving drugs?"

"Well, in those days drugs like cocaine and heroine were part of the scene and I was aware that odd ones were sniffing it outside the pub. But as long as they didn't cause any bother in the pub I turned a blind eye. However, I can honestly say I have never touched any of the revolting stuff in my life. The reason for this is because of something that happened to me when I was just ten years old. Drugs were just appearing on the scene and I seemed destined to become an addict. But then, my brother's best friend died of an overdose and that incident imbedded something into my brain that drugs were wrong. Luckily for me I had never indulged in any kind of drugs and I have never taken anything in my life since then. I've done most things in life and nothing shocks me anymore ... I've got the 'T' shirt and worn it. I have certainly been a piss artist but I have never ever taken a powder, a pill or any other type of the poisonous crap."

"You appear to have enjoyed the pub life... why did you pack it in?"

"Well, sadly, on the morning of January 14th 2013 I didn't feel well at all. Tracey, my partner, knew there was something wrong and rang for an ambulance. After tests at the hospital I was diagnosed with a mild stroke and also the onset of diabetes. From then on my world changed. Tracey finished up being my carer. Fortunately, I wasn't left with a crippling disability but it definitely slowed me down. It left me with no option but to give up the pub. For a while after I just moped about the house and got quite depressed just thinking about what I could do. Then I got to know about Darren, who ran a poker competition every Thursday night at the Dugdale Arms. It turned out well because I made friends of the many characters who enjoy the game. I realised that poker is a good socialiser and bring all kinds of people together on an even keel. I met up with people from all walks of life and we all gelled together as one happy family. I have been a regular player ever since and I always look forward to the event."

"I know where you're coming from Luggy … I feel the same. Finally Luggy, how do you feel about pocket aces?"

"To put it mildly I don't like the bloody things … I've lost more chips with them than any other cards. I don't mess about with 'em any more … I just go All In before the flop so as to stop anyone getting two pair with rag arse cards. On saying that, I once finished up with quad aces and a player went All In. I called and said I had two large pairs. He had a nut flush and as he happily went to scoop up the pot I laughed and pointed out that they were two pairs of aces. To say the least … he wasn't very pleased. He actually came out with language that even made my hair curl."

"Ha ha! That's hard to believe>"

****

I found all Luggy's tales to be interesting, funny and even poignant including the one when he lost all his teeth. It was tragic … yet hilarious.

Due to the Corona Virus all poker events were closed down for a few months. On re-opening … Luggy won the first competition at the Ighten Leigh Club … what a good do!

CHAPTER 5 - ALL-IN ANDREW

I got in touch with Andrew Hennessey and asked him if he would like to be a character in the book.

"Of course I would Tas," he responded enthusiastically, "I'd love it!"

"Great Andy, I'm glad about that because I think your story will be interesting. I know you're in the building trade as you have done a job for me."

"That's right Tas, and after a hard day's grind I so look forward to a game of poker ... it really relaxes me."

"You know something Andy ... that's what everybody says."

After the phone call we got together and talked about the game. Andrew loves poker and is known amongst his poker buddies as 'All In Andrew.

"I know it's obvious why you got tagged with that nickname, but tell me a little more about it." I asked.

"Well what it is John, in the first hour before the break I know I can re-buy more chips so I think, 'Oh what the hell!' I often go All-In blind simply to get others to bet and boost up the pot." He paused a little and then laughed heartily, "It doesn't half get up some players' noses when I beat them and especially when I get a hand like 6/3 and come up with two pair."

"Aye Andrew, and I bet they're pleased with you."

"You can say that again." he laughed, "You jammy bastard! followed by a few 'f' words."

"Ha, ha, I can imagine."

"Yeah you imagine right Tas. Anyway, sometimes I do it simply because I am getting bored with my holding cards hoping to get a change of luck."

"That's alright ... but don't you think that players will get used to your tactics?"

"Maybe but, then again, that's part of my plan. I don't want people to get comfortable playing nice and safe. I get them out of their comfort zone and this frustrates them. It works for me as I seem to get lucky using this method. Even with low cards I seem to fare well against an ace or a picture card."

I had to smile at that remark, "You can say that again, ... I've seen you do it against pocket aces!"

You may think I'm wild but I'm not a loose cannon altogether. My strategy is to try my luck in the first hour before the break and try to build up a good stack of chips. My plan is to capitalise by tightening up a little after the break and players still think I'm in a loose mood When I've been in a hand that I knew was a positive winner I've often told my opponent to fold their hand. But to my advantage, they never believe me and I rake in a stack of chips.

"Ha ha! That's funny! Anyway Andrew, how do you fare overall?"

"Well he smiled, I do have an occasional win but, like everybody else, not as often as I would like."

"Yeah it's a funny game, it does seem to go around in circles."

It does that but overall I love the game because it gives me a break from my working life and really puts me at ease. It's a great way of meeting a variety of people and I thoroughly enjoy the social aspect of it."

"Do you know something ... that's what everybody says about the game."

"Aye and there's something else about it. I've made many good friends amongst the poker players. And that's not just socially ... I've had some good working contacts like the job I did for you."

"Yeah thanks Andrew ... you did a good job too."

Andrew stroked his chin again in deep thought and then continued, "The magical thing about poker is that you're going to have good luck when you're flying and bad luck when you're back on your heels. We all sit around the table and feel the elation when a player scoops up a good pot and likewise, we feel the controlled agony when they take a beating."-

"Aye, I know what you mean ... it's a feeling from one extreme to the other."

"Another thing that's good is that youngsters like the game as well. Some of them drink a lot and get rather merry. But then again, they've worked hard all week and they're just letting their hair down ... it's all part of their night out."

We chatted a little more about the intriguing game and then he told me a little about his personal life.

"Right then, where do I start?" he said deep in thought. Going back to my childhood it was a far cry from nowadays. That may sound like a cliché as you may have heard that expression many times. I recall my first day at school and all the parents were there. A boy approached me and offered me a toffee. His father, a school teacher, had prompted him because he firmly believed on the importance of connecting with people and making friends. He must have thought I was a suitable candidate. The boy's name was Paul and we became best friends throughout our school life. I lived at the top entrance to Scott's Park and Paul lived at the lower entrance. Living so close to each other I called for him every day after school and also at weekends. We spent many hours in the park making dens and getting up to tomfoolery. A river ran through the park and we used to make dams and set traps for the unsuspecting park ranger. We got up to loads of mischief and even smashed up garages at the back of his house.

"Did the park ranger ever catch you Andrew?"

"Ha ha!" he laughed, "No we were far too fast for him."

"It's happen as well, because when I was a kid I used to frequent the same park and I know the house well where he lived ... it was on the left corner plot as you entered the park from Albion Street. Mind you, in my childhood he was called a park keeper and he always carried a long stick which he'd crack you with if he caught you,"

Andrew cracked up laughing again, "Yeah, but, like I said, we never got caught. Anyway, another favourite of ours was smashing bottles. We'd line them up on a wall, four or five at a time, and throw stones at them from about ten yards away. At one time we acquired an air pistol and we'd hide in thick bushes and fire at people passing by and then leg it. Ha ha! .... Usain Bolt wouldn't have caught us."

"U-um, you were quite naughty then ... even to the point of being bad. It's happen as well Paul's dad didn't find out with him being a teacher."

"Aye you're right there. That reminds me ... his dad must have thought I was under-nourished because every time I went to his house he always offered me something to eat."

"Ha ha, you don't look under nourished now Andrew. Anyway you and Paul seemed to be good buddies."

"Yeah we were but there was one time when I got quite jealous. It was Christmas and he got a present that I desperately wanted ... it was an 'Etch a Sketch'. At the time, to me, it was a technological marvel. Mind you, I soon got over it. Another hobby of ours was collecting comics. I liked the Beano but he preferred the Dandy. I built up quite an impressive collection and I kept each issue in pristine condition."

"You know something Andy, I used to love the Beano as well with Biffo the Bear on the front cover."

Andrew frowned for a moment and then said, "I'll tell you something now John that I'm not proud of. My mum always had her hands full looking after me and my sisters. Despite her plight I once took a fifty pence piece from her purse and bought a large bar of Toblerone from the corner shop. On my way home I became overcome with guilt and wasn't sure what to do. I decided to put it in a place where I could spot it from our kitchen window. I later pretended to be excited and I called Mum over saying that someone must have dropped a chocolate bar. I then rushed outside and picked up my booty and, on entering the home, I offered my mum a piece. Mum was very canny and I'm sure she knew something was going on but, luckily for me, she never said anything. I never did anything like that again and I strived to make it up to mum in many different ways after that."

"That's good ... we all do things that we later regret. Anyway Andrew, how did you fare at school?"

"Personally John, I always thought school was a complete waste of time and I used to skive off it at every opportunity. When I was there I was quite disruptive. I remember my parents being totally shocked after attending a parents' meeting just prior to me leaving junior school. They were informed not to build their hopes up for me as I would never amount to anything. Consequently, when I went to senior school, they put me in the lowest class amongst all the dunces. I wasn't happy about it at all and felt strongly that something was wrong. But deep down I knew that it was my own fault and I was determined to do something about it. I got my head down and, twice running, I came top of the class. My improvement was noted and the following term I was moved up two streams and back in a class alongside my friends.

"Well done ... but how did you cope in that class?"

"Well, in the third year I was told to report to the headmaster, Mr Duxbury, and he informed me that he thought I was a border line genius and said I should feel privileged to be offered the chance of becoming a priest. He also said I was one of life's natural leaders and where I went others would willingly follow. I politely pointed out that there was no way that I wanted to join the priesthood. He tried to change my mind but there was no chance."

"There's one thing for sure Andrew, they'd certainly changed their tune about you."

"Aye you can say that again. Anyroad, whilst we're on about school I'll tell you about one of my many playground fights and it was a bloody affair. One particular bully kept goading me and one day he went too far. I was rather nervous as he had a renowned reputation, but I knew I had to lay my ghost to rest and tackle my problem head on. The fight was arranged for during the dinner break behind the canteen and word of it quickly spread around the school yard. I'd been forewarned that he was a dirty fighter and I remember thinking that I couldn't afford to let him get in the first blow. But that was easier said than done as, he was not only as strong as an ox but he was quick footed as well. After exchanging a few vicious blows we finished up grappling on the ground. We were well both matched but I gradually got the better of him. I grabbed him by his hair and tried to pound his head to the floor but he in turn tried to claw my eyes out. During the gruesome encounter blood started to flow down my face. In desperation I pummelled his head to the ground even more brutally and, thankfully, he said he'd had enough. He was a mess but so was I with a busted nose and one 'eck of a black eye and scratches down my face. Hence, when we both turned up for registration all battered and worn the teacher noticed immediately and ordered us to the front of the class. We both denied any wrong doings ... it was a kind of 'Code of Honour'. Luckily we didn't get reprimanded and the teacher let it go at that. After that fight, nobody messed about with me anymore. In fact I became a kind of protector for some of the meek and mild students."

"That's interesting Andrew. It seems that you were starting to enjoy school life."

"Well it was better but the only thing I liked during my school days were the PE sessions ... I was well into keeping fit. At one time I organised a cycling session and about twelve of us went out for a bike ride around country lanes. After that it became a regular occurrence but I still couldn't wait to leave school."

"And did you go into the building trade straight away?"

"Yeah, but I didn't stick to one trade in particular ... I guess you could call me a Jack of all trades'. But, when I was in my early twenties my cousin Clare introduced me to her boyfriend, Jonathan Green. He lived in the biggest house in Burnley in the Prairie district ... it was called Brompton House. It was bounded by a high stone wall with electronic gates and the back of the house had a panoramic view of Pendle Hill and the surrounding countryside."

"Oh I remember the place well Andy ... there was an article written up about it in the Burnley Express. It was the first ever house in Burnley to be worth over fifty thousand pounds. I recall looking at it from Colne Road and it was set way back in acres of land with a large driveway. It was built similar to a Spanish villa and was referred to locally as 'The Ponderosa', which translates to 'Powerful'. It was a beautiful place but it has since been demolished in the name of progress and replaced by a large enclosed football field.

"Yeah, that's the one. Anyway I got on really well with Jonathan and, together with Clare, and my girlfriend, we all went to the south of France. At the time I had a Honda van and so I did the driving. We hadn't planned anything special and just lived the simple life ... it was great."

"Ha, ha! I laughed, "Holidaying in the south of France ... it appears more than a simple life to me."

"Yeah, maybe. Anyway, things carried on in a similar vein and then Jonathan and his father got done for drug smuggling. They'd been trafficking cannabis on a large scale from South Africa for quite a while. They'd built up their enterprise by smuggling 50 kilogram packages through customs wrapped in sheepskins. On being found guilty, Jonathan received a six year sentence and his dad was sent down for ten years. The law was different at the time and, any property bought by ill-gotten gains could not be confiscated by the police. And it wasn't just the house. In a large double garage there was a Rolls Royce, a Mercedes Benz and a sports car."

"Oh I remember the incident well Andy ... it was plastered in all the newspapers and on television. Also it was the first time I'd heard about drug trafficking in Burnley"

"Aye you're right there."

"What happened after that ... did you keep in contact with them?"

"U-um, did I! Jonathan asked me to look after his mother whilst he and his dad were in prison. I felt obligated and promised him I would. So I kept popping round to the house to keep an eye on her and also to do little jobs about the place. Things were going smooth until one day when I went to the house and the old lady was in a right state ... she was really distraught."

"How come?"

"Well, a Geordie thug who she knew well, had broken into the home and forced her to hand over the keys to the

Mercedes. Leaving her in a helpless state he then drove the car away."

"Oh I think I know what's coming now ... you felt responsible eh?"

"I did that. I'd made a promise that I'd take care of her and I felt as though I had let her down."

"But that wasn't your fault ... there was nothing you could do about it."

"That's where you're wrong. I asked her if she knew where the bloke lived and she gave me an address in Newcastle. I made my mind up there and then that I would retrieve the car at any cost."

"Bloomin' 'eck Andrew, it seems to me you were treading on dangerous ground messing about with drug dealers."

"Yeah, maybe I was but I was determined to get the car back for her. The lady forewarned me that he was a very nasty, dangerous character but I didn't care ... I just had to keep to the promise I'd made to her son."

"This is getting interesting ... how did you go about it?"

"Well I found the place and the car was parked in a long driveway. A night light was on and, as I approached the house, an alarm went off. Within a minute, a huge fierce looking chap appears asking who the fuck I am. I told him

I'd come to take the car back. The next thing I know he is running at me wielding a baseball bat and bellowing, 'Like fuck you are!'"

"Blimey ... I'd have been outa there like a bat out of hell."

"I've got to admit ... that thought did cross my mind. But luckily for me he stumbled and, as he tried to get up, I kicked him in the head. Despite a bust nose he got up and we were having a right scrap knocking ten bells o' crap out of each other. I was getting the better of him and then his wife clobbered me with the baseball bat splitting my head wide open. Blood ran down my face and I could only see out of one eye, but my adrenaline was running. I dragged her like a rag doll and clobbered her. I then picked up a brick and was going to whack him with it. But then he just put his hands up with his fingers open wide and said, 'Take the fucking car ... just get outa here!' Like all thugs ... he was a coward. The front door was wide open so I cockily walked into the kitchen and wiped my face with a towel. The woman followed me, offered me the car keys and murmured ... 'Just go!'"

"So your little escapade was all done and dusted ... but what about your own car that you'd driven up there in?"

"Well, I'd parked it not too far from that house and I later had to catch a train in order to get it."

"Was that your final dealing with the underworld?"

"No, in fact it was just the beginning. Her husband was grateful for what I had done and, even though he was in jail, he spread the word about me to the underground. Things quickly stepped up a gear and I was contacted by a firm in Manchester. I got employed by a few ruffians and, if someone needed sorting out, they got in touch with yours truly. From then on I travelled the length and breadth of the country. I sorted a few thugs out but never anyone who was undeserving and I drew the line at sheer thuggery. And, there were certain ganglands that I steered well clear of."

He paused a little before continuing, "Right, now Tas ... a bit of my working life. I've got to say that I'm a pretty laid back sort of a fellow, but I do take my working life very seriously. Whereas lots of people hate having to go out to work every day and find it a bind ... I consider myself very lucky because I love my work."

"That's good Andrew ... it reminds me of an old proverb, 'Show me a man happy in his work and I will show you a happy man'".

"Yeah, I guess that about weighs me up. I have a variety of jobs and I'll tackle almost anything in the building trade, but I always aim to do my very best. Of course, the money is important but I always get a kick out of it when a customer is well pleased with the outcome. To me ... that's an added bonus."

"I think you have a nice outlook on life Andy."

"I like to think so ... it makes me happy. The way I look at it, we're only here for a short time on this earth and we should always strive to do our best. When I walk away from a job I like to think I have done my best. That's how I choose to spend my life."

I was impressed by his attitude to life.

"A few years ago," he carried on with his tale, "I bought an old hotel and converted it to a house. My intention was to accommodate my family should they struggle with the overbearing tension of everyday modern living. I just wanted to take the stress of paying scandalous high over rated rents off their shoulders. I also didn't like the thought of my elderly father living on his own and so he moved in with us. He was with us for six years but sadly, he died at the age of ninety-two."

"E-eh Andy, I'll bet you missed him ... my mother died at the age of ninety-one and I sure as 'eck miss her."

"Yeah I did. Anyway, currently living in our home are my wife Amanda and I, two daughters, a son, a 'son-in-law', five grandchildren and one of my son's friends.

"By 'eck Andrew, twelve in one house ... you've certainly got your hands full."

"You can say that again but I love it … I wouldn't change it for the world. I also have another daughter who lives in London and I have a special room with an en suite for her when she visits us."

"All I can say Andy … your wife must be a busy lady."

Yeah, Amanda basically runs the home and makes most of the important decisions. However, it's great to be part of a busy household. It's like living on 'Walton's Mountain' and there's never a dull moment."

"I can imagine," I smiled, "and, when your dad was alive, it would have been good for him watching all the antics of his great grandchildren."

"Yeah, it was, but it' was good for me as well."

Once again he paused before telling me about a down side in his life.

"Years ago I grafted hard and ventured into buying old houses and doing them up. I sold the odd one but rented out most of them. At one time I had built up a great portfolio and, on paper, I was a rich man. A large enterprise became very interested in my project and offered me £7 million for my entire stock. I thought about it and foolishly declined the offer, as in the previous year my gross turnover was almost a million pounds. I later regretted my decision, but then again it's easy to be wise with retrospect. Sadly, for me, the following year there was a bank recession and the housing market collapsed. The bank was ruthless and called in all my assets and charged me ever spiralling interest on my overdraft. Consequently I had to sell off my properties individually at deflated prices and lost an enormous amount of money. The incident obviously knocked me off my feet and I felt rather down in the dumps. But then my resilience kicked in and I got stuck in again."

"Good for you Andy ... good on you! Did you still stay in the building trade?"

"Yeah. In fact, I bought another house to rent out and it was on Piccadilly Road, in Burnley and I rented it out to a decent looking couple. Renting a house out isn't all it's cracked up to be. If you get a good tenant then it's great but, if you get a bad one, it can be hell. Despite references, you can never tell what a tenant is going to be like until they've actually moved into the house."

"Aye, I agree with you there Andy ... I've had a few bad tenants myself in my time."

"Anyway, this so called decent couple turned out to be junkies."

"Don't say they trashed the house!"

"No, to be fair they didn't but it was hard work getting the rent off them. They were on social and instead of the council sending me the rent they sent it to them. This meant that I had to be on the ball every month to make sure I was at the house to make sure they didn't spend it "

"U-um, it's crazy why the council do that instead of sending it directly to the landlord."

"Yeah, that's the Council isn't it? Anyway John, one little tale I'd like to tell you. I was there one day and the husband asked me if I would like to buy a diamond ring. He then opened a showcase box lined with green satin and inside were a few diamond rings. It appeared to me that the rings had been stolen from a jeweller's shop. He showed me one that he said was worth a thousand pounds and offered it to me for £300. It looked absolutely fantastic and, as greed took over, I handed him the money. But, to make sure I was not being conned, I took it to a dealer and had it valued. Alas, he informed me that it was paste and practically worthless. I went back to the house in a flash and threatened to throttle the bloke if he didn't give me my money back. But it was too late ... the money had already been spent. However, he did come up with another proposition. He offered me another ring which he swore was worth £2000 and even volunteered to go along with me to have it valued. But he said the deal was to keep the ring as security and he would buy it back from me in a month's time for the £300 he owed me. Well, a month passed and he actually came up with the money but I told him I had lost the ring. He was a bit pissed off but he couldn't do anything about it."

"Ha ha Andy, so instead of him conning you, you conned him!"

"Too right I did ... it served him bloody well right. The way I saw it was that he'd tried to swindle me but his little scam backfired on him."

****

He then went on to tell me about other schemes he had up his sleeve. "Besides the building trade," he said, "I have another mode of thinking. What it is ... I am forever conjuring up ideas and designing various objects which, in my opinion, would make a bomb. But every time I try to explain my idea to anyone, no matter how many times I go over it, they can't grasp the concept how of it works. Not to worry, one of these days I'm going to get one of my gadgets patented so I'll have total copyright and then they'll prick up their ears and listen.

"Ha, ha ... you do that Andy!"

CHAPTER 6 - JAMES

I visit James' house frequently as his mother is my twin sister. It was on one of my visits that James and I discussed the book. Like all the other characters he loves the game of poker and thinks it is magical how it brings people together.

"What I'm after James is a brief outline of your life," I told him.

For obvious reasons I knew about his child upbringing but I wanted to glean some of his army life and thereafter.

"Right Uncle John ... here goes. As a child I lived in Rosegrove in Burnley, a Lancashire town set amongst many tall factory chimneys when cotton mills, weaving sheds and coal mines were still up and running. I was the youngest of four children having two brothers, Michael and Dale, and a sister, Avril. We lived in a small three bedroom terraced house in the middle of the block. Avril had her own bedroom whereas I had to share one with my two brothers. We were constantly battling for space and, needless to say, I lost out every time."

"I know where you're coming from there James because I too had to share a bedroom too with my two brothers when I was a lad."

"Yeah, right, that would have been my Uncle Jimmy and Uncle Barry wouldn't it?"

"Right in one."

"Anyway Uncle John, I'll carry on. Rosegrove was like a small village and everybody knew each other. Men spent lots of time in the pubs and women had to work full time as well as looking after the household. My mum was a real fighter and plodded on relentlessly to give us whatever we needed but there was never anything left over for luxuries. I was an outdoor person and well into the sporting scene. Football and cricket were my favourites but I was also into table tennis and snooker. Luckily, there were numerous youth clubs around town and I spent many hours in lots of them."

"That reminds me of my teenage years James ... but I think it's a shame for today's youth as there's not many of these facilities around anymore."

"Aye you're right there. Anyway Uncle John, like you know, my mum never had much money and she could only afford to give us ten pence a week spending money. Unlike many of my friends I never did get to go on a holiday. During the summer holidays I spent many hours moping about and burning tarmac near the kerb with a magnifying glass and sticking match and lollipop sticks into it."

"Ha ha, I used to do the same with gas tar in between the stone cobbles on Albion Street when I was a lad."

James laughed a little and then came out with a little confession. "Do you know something Uncle John, I did something very wrong when I was in my teens. I was in the 'Boy's Brigade' and it had organised a two week trip to France. I broached Mum about it but she simply couldn't come up with the money. I was gutted ... I'd never ever had a holiday in my life but I was determined to have this one. Hence, I forged a sponsorship form stating that I was going to walk many miles on the Leeds and Liverpool Canal. My scam worked and I collected enough money to go on the trip and have a little spending money. I thoroughly enjoyed the break but after returning home I was filled with guilt as I knew I had done something very wrong. I realised that integrity is the best policy and I vowed never to do anything untoward again."

"Not to worry James ... we've all done something that we shouldn't have at one time in our lives. Anyway tell me a bit more about Michael and Dale."

I was a happy kid and contented with my lot but, being the youngest of four, I soon learned to 'get smart' and keep out of the way. My two brothers and I spent many hours at Gannow Baths and they constantly tried to drown me. Hence, I quickly learned to swim and I kept out of their way in the deep end. Around my sixteenth birthday my eldest brother Michael joined the army. He was a fantastic footballer and became an obvious choice to play for 'Tri Services' which was the highest accolade for football in the forces.

"I know he was a great footballer James, because I regularly watched him play in Towneley Park. I saw him score one of the best goals I have ever seen in my life. He was way over on the left wing and he floated a ball right into the top corner of the net leaving the goalkeeper with no chance. Anyway you joined the army shortly after that. Was it because of Michael?"

"Yeah it was. Dale and I both wanted to join him to escape the droll life in Burnley."

"Oh. I didn't realise Dale wanted to join the army as well. How come he never went in with you?"

"Well what it is ... after the initial interview the recruitment officer turned our Dale down because he had tattoos on his hands. He was devastated but he still encouraged me to go for it. I felt gutted for him because he'd so looked forward to it. Still, I took his advice and, before I knew it, I was on a train heading for Harrogate. On disembarking, there were three Bedford army four-ton trucks waiting to pick up 180 new recruits."

"How did you feel at that moment?"

"To put it mildly I was scared. It appeared to be a total mishmash and I can only describe it as a 'What the hell' moment. Amongst the group were many skinheads wearing Harrington jackets, skin tight jeans and Doc Marten boots. I felt nervous but, a giant of a lad next to me was shaking like an aspen leaf. It turned out he was from the Isle of Skye and it was his first ever time away from home. Because of his demeanour I felt a little bit more at ease. Lots of other guys appeared nervous as well, but there were a few cocky ones putting on the bravado act."

"Did that bother you?"

"Aye, it did a bit but then again I've always been pretty good at sizing folk up ... especially bullies."

"What about the skinheads?"

"I've got to admit I weighed them up wrong because most of them turned out to be really nice guys and good mates whereas the big nervous lad from Skye became a real maniac when he was riled."

"So after your initiation how did you go on in camp?"

It was great. During my two years training at Harrogate I was well into keeping fit. I played regular football and cricket and I also took up boxing. Things were going great and then something happened that ripped my stomach out."

"Oh I think I know what's coming ... it was our Michael wasn't it?"

"Yeah, you're right Uncle John. The sergeant major got me up in the middle of the night and marched me across the parade ground to the commandant's office where I was informed that my brother had died on a football field. When I asked which one he didn't know. I knew that our Dale had gone off the rails and was into drugs so I automatically thought it was him. I didn't find out until I was back home in Burnley that it was our Michael ... I was in complete shock."

"U-um, I know exactly how you felt ... we were all devastated by the news back here at home.. I thought our Mary, your mum, was going to have a complete breakdown ... especially at the funeral. As far as the event went the army did him proud and gave him a full military funeral and you looked magnificent in your dress uniform. Still it was a very sad affair and nobody could quite take it in that he had just collapsed on a football field and died."

"Yeah, it was an awful time Uncle John ... it threw the entire family into complete chaos. I was just seventeen and our Michael was only twenty-one ... it just didn't seem real. It took me a few years to come to terms with it and then I was knocked back again when our Dale also died at the age of twenty-six. In a way it was half expected as by now he was heavily into drugs. But the fact remains that he was my brother and it still hit me hard. I always felt on my own and isolated after that ... and especially so in the years to come when I was back in 'Civvy Street'."

"I can imagine you did our James ... I can imagine you did!"

"Anyway, reflecting back on my army days and my first mission abroad in Germany, my very first night was a real eye opener. I was a non-drinker and intended to have a quiet night in. But, I'd no sooner unpacked my kit bag when a bunch of blokes burst into my billet, grabbed me and carried me across to the 'NAAFI CLUB'. They'd already shanghaied four of my mates and we were informed that it was an initiation and that we had to play a game of 'Schock Dice'. Several shots of whisky and other cocktails later, I found myself falling about and writhing on the parade ground and spilling my guts up."

"Ha ha, a similar thing happened to me when I joined the army ... I didn't touch whisky for years after that."

"No, neither did I. Anyway, I gradually settled in well, made lots of friends and I undertook a 'Senior Army Kayak Instructor Course' and was trained by an RSM who was an Olympic medallist. I gradually became the main instructor in the entire British Army and took trainees out onto the open sea and also kayaked down many white water rapids. A challenge was thrown up and together, with a crew of sixteen, we canoed the entire length of the River Rhine from Basil in Switzerland to Rotterdam in Holland. It was an amazing feat which took us nearly two weeks slogging away both day and night through smooth water and white water rapids. During the escapade we took turns at rowing whilst others tried to get their head down. On reaching Rotterdam, the Rhine was about a mile wide and, due to angry underwater currents, we found it difficult to keep out of the way of many massive tankers blasting their fog horns."

"Like you said James it was an amazing feat."

"Aye it was that. Anyway, we decided to celebrate in the renowned city but went way over the top. After a few bevvies we got into a brawl with some rough looking blokes and finished up in a police cell with guns held against our heads. To say the least ...... it was bloody scary."

"I bet it was. At least it was a good tale to share with your mates."

"You're not kidding. Anyway back at camp another regiment challenged us to a boxing match. Our team was made up of nine men and each one of us had to do three, three minute rounds and try to knock the hell out of our opponents. On reaching a large gym it was packed to capacity and drums were beating loudly. After eight bouts the score was even at 4-4, and I was the last contestant for our team. I couldn't stop my knees from shaking and I must have gone to the toilet ten times. The trouble is I had my boxing gloves on and my mates had to keep pulling out my 'Little Jimmy' to guide it to the pisspot. My opponent was taller than me with a muscular frame and he scared the crap out of me. But I remember muttering to myself, 'Oh what the hell ... go for it!' This I did and do you know what ... I knocked the bloke out in the first minute. My team mates went wild and carried me out of the gym with the sound of 'Gre-e-at, resounding around the room ... I was a hero."

"I can imagine ... I bet it was a great feeling."

"As a reward for winning the trophy our team got a 72 hour pass and six of us flew over to England and spent a great night in Doncaster. Another guy from our camp, but not in our team, persuaded us to stop over an extra night. He convinced us all that we would be treated leniently if we all said that the train was delayed. Being young and foolish we all agreed. But it didn't go to plan. As soon as we passed through the camp gates we were all arrested and thrown in the brig. All of us that is except the bloke who'd talked us into it."

"How come ... why did he not get arrested too?"

"Well, the slimy bastard just pulled out an authorisation slip stating he had another day's leave due. He just glanced at us and said, 'have fun guys'. What sort of prank is that?"

"Blimey James, from what I can remember about my army days, he wouldn't have been very popular after that amongst the troops."

"Aye you're right there ... he certainly rued the day he pulled his sick joke for months after that."

"U-um, I can well imagine. Anyroad, what happened to you and your mates?"

"Well we all got sentenced to four days in the nick with loss of pay. We had to scrub floors in the sergeants' mess on our hands and knees, clean loads of greasy pots and pans and get regular beatings. Believe me Uncle John even the toughest of men wouldn't want to go into that hell house twice."

"Ha ha, I know where you're coming from James ... I've been there."

****

Another time, seven buddies and I, had to do a field exercise under battle conditions and the point of the activity was to avoid being ambushed. I was in charge of our platoon and we planned it well but, unbeknown to us, it

211

was a set up. We were overthrown by a squad of ten commandos led by a very aggressive sergeant major, who'd been trained to capture and torture us. After being taken prisoners they stripped us bollock naked, put a hessian sack bag over our heads, tied our hands behind our backs and bound our feet. They then grabbed us and man handled us into a four ton Bedford truck. We were driven to a prison type building and thrown onto a concrete floor. We could hear screams, coming from another room, of someone being tortured. It was a mind game ... they were using tapes but we didn't know it at the time. Each one of us in turn was taken to a basement that was three feet deep in muddy water and thrown in. We all finished up like clay men and they left us lying in a cold dank room for ages. I managed to stand up with my face against a wall. One of my mates was very agile and he managed to kneel down and loosen my binds with his teeth. It appeared as if we were making a pornographic movie. Once my hands were free I then freed all of my buddies and we put a plan into action. We all started moaning and screaming for a medic and, luckily for us, there was only the sergeant major outside our cell. When he opened the cell door we all charged forward and trampled him to the ground leaving him in a semi-conscious state. Once outside we sprinted across some grassland into a thick wood. Eventually we came across a farmhouse which we ransacked. We cut up a luxury carpet and used remnants as shoes and used the hessian to make loin cloths. Now paraded like Stone Age men we traipsed through thick foliage to make our way back to camp. About three hours later the area was swarming with Land Rovers with speakers announcing that the exercise was over. But we didn't reveal ourselves as we thought it was a ploy. It was only when our own sergeant major informed us over a loud speaker that we came out into the open. We were later informed that we had passed the test and actually got a pat on the back for compromising and improvising under battle conditions.

"Bloody hell James ... they went a bit over the top didn't they?"

"Aye you're right there, but it was good practice and put us in good stead later when we were posted abroad to places like Kuwait, Cyprus for the UN peacekeepers and Northern Ireland."

****

"My real claim to fame is when Iraq invaded Kuwait, which resulted in a seven month long occupation of the country. The Iraqi military set fire to over six hundred oil wells. Saddam Hussein invaded on 10 Aug 1990 and I was the first detachment commander to arrive in Seeb, Oman. I, along with my detachment, had been on standby and highly trained for such an event. We had to set up and secure communications in readiness for the RAF, a regiment of US marines and other units to arrive. In total, I was stationed there for almost seven months and was witness to some of my mates being killed during the conflict."

"I remember it well James, it was headline news back here at home and your mother was fretting her heart out knowing you were in the thick of it. What was the morale like amongst the soldiers?"

"It was good because lots of famous celebrities used to come over from America to entertain the troops. I remember Steve Martin in particular because I had to push myself through a crowd to get his autograph. My sergeant major bollocked me and then gave a sly wink and said, 'Get one for me as well Clancy!' That's what it was like. The camaraderie and banter amongst the troops was second to none. We had our arguments but when it came to the crunch we backed each other up to the hilt,

"It seems like you enjoyed your army life James."

"Well I've got to admit it was a good experience and I made a lot of good mates."

****

"I spent a little time in Norway and had a brilliant time. One afternoon, along with my mates, we tried to spot a fat girl, and when we did, we started to take the piss out of

214

her. To our surprise she turned and called us a load of wankers and said she was from Manchester. She joined us and we had a fantastic night."

"E-eh, you can't beat a Lancashire lass."

"Aye, you're right there. Anyroad, another night we had a ladies night for charity. A few of us dressed up as drag queens and we had to walk on a catwalk like a model. A gigantic lad, weighing about nineteen stone was dressed as a ballet dancer. He was as pissed as a fart and kept flipping over on his high heels flashing his all. Oh my God ... it was hilarious! Then another lad came onto the catwalk wearing fishnets. He looked gorgeous and all the ladies loved it. It was the best laugh I had had for ages and to make it better the event raised quite a lot of money for the charity."

****

I was later to learn that James had received four medals during his army career from serving in The Gulf War - Northern Ireland - Kuwait and a special one from 'The United Nations.'

"Did you miss army life when you were demobbed into Civvy Street?" I asked."

"I did in a way because in the army a lot of life's problems are taken off your shoulders. On leaving the army I studied and kind of slid into Financial Services as an

Independent Financial Adviser. I got married and had two girls and they became my world. I now had a wife, two children, a mortgage and the responsibility of putting food on the table. I was now beginning to feel the pressure and stress of life's problems. But, as I got on well with folk, I hit my targets and made a decent living. I especially remember one client for obvious reasons ... he wanted to invest one hundred million pounds. It was one of those once in a lifetime opportunities, accountants and solicitors became involved during negotiations. Nevertheless, sadly for me, they couldn't reach an agreement on the commission rate and my client backed out."

"Oh, what a shame ... I'll bet you was gutted."

"U-umph, you can bet I was. Anyway, I still did all right and in between work I spent lots of time with my family and we went on expensive holidays to places like Mexico and Florida. Whenever I had time on my hands I spent it with my little princesses ... my life was a dream."

"E-eh, that was nice. And now my question is ... how did you get onto the poker scene?"

"Ah well as you know, I used to play lots of card games in the Junction Pub and about fourteen years ago I got to know about Darren running a poker club. I got in touch and I've been playing it ever since ... I love it. What's good about it is that there is always a great atmosphere

216

with people taking the piss out of each other. Usually, about thirty odd players join in the game and there's loads of characters from all walks of life, including women. It's a barrel of laughs listening to different tales."

"I know what you mean ... especially listening to players like Luggy Did you pick up on all the expressions pretty quickly like flop, river, fishing etc ...?"

"Yeah, what a laugh. I saw players making bets and getting upset by bluffers who were fishing and came up trumps on the river. Before the break, some guys gamble all their chips knowing too well that they can always re-buy and have another fish."

"Do you bluff James?"

"Yeah, course I do ... it's all part and parcel of the game isn't it?"

"Do you remember any special event in particular?"

"I do that ... it's the 'Goliath,' a yearly event held in Coventry. It's the biggest poker event in the world after the World Series in Las Vegas."

"Yeah, I go along with you there ... I've only been once but what an event."

"Anyway, another thing I like about poker is that there's lots of respect shown between young and old alike. But it's not for the fainthearted as funny expressions spring to mind.

"You jammy bastard!"

"What the fuck!"

"Wanker!"

"You lucky shit!"

And, "Fuckin' lesbian!" always creates a laugh."

"Ha ha!" I laughed, "Right, one last question ... can you remember any particular hand that springs to mind?"

"Oh, I can that. My two holding cards were pocket aces and the flop was A/10/10."

"Wow, a full house on the flop ... that's a dream hand."

"Yeah, that's what I thought, but my dream was nearly shattered. I'd 30000 chips in front of me and I bet 10000. A player not only called me but he went all in."

"Great, that's what you wanted isn't it?"

"Yeah, of course I did and I obviously went all in with him. I was dead chuffed until he turned his two cards over to reveal pocket tens ... I couldn't believe it."

"Four of a kind ... what a knockback. But then again, you just said that your dream was nearly shattered."

"Yeah, that's right. Believe it or not the turn card was a three of hearts and the river was .... The **Ace of Clubs!** Wo-ow! I gleefully scooped up a load of chips whilst my opponent just looked on in disbelief moaning, 'You jammy spawny lucky bastard!!"

****

Overall, James is a very good player and his game is solid. To my Knowledge he has won the comp at the Dugdale Arms and Ighten Leigh Club on several occasions. I remember one in particular because it was my eightieth birthday. We were heads up and he had a slightly higher stack than me. He went 'All In' and I called with A/J. He had pocket nines and they carried him through to beat me.

Every Christmas, Darren runs a special comp where the winner receives a trophy and gets his name inscribed onto a winner's shield. Christmas 2000, James not only won the medal and prize money of £680, but at the end of the night he also won a one-off game where every player put £20 into the pot and he scooped the lot. He went home with 960 pounds in his pocket ... what a good start to the Christmas break.

He has also won the league on at least two occasions which takes some doing. He's definitely a player to be wary of.

CHAPTER 7 - PROCKY

P rocky is one of the regulars of the Thursday night brigade and he is the guy who organises the Bounty. He's as keen on poker as anybody I have come across ... and he's certainly a shrewd player. He called me over one night in the club and said he'd love to be a character in the book.

"That's great Procky, I'm sure you'll have a few good tales to tell."

"I have that Tas ... if I bared my soul you could write three books."

"Great! That's exactly the sort of stuff I'm after. Anyroad, are you a Burnley lad?"

"Yeah I am. My mum was only sixteen when she got pregnant with me and she had six brothers and seven sisters. She was a single mum and all her brothers ganged up on her fella and told him, in no uncertain terms, to either marry my mum or get out of town."

"And what did he do?"

"He chose the latter and shot off to Australia."

"So, did your mum ever see him again?"

No, but news came back over the grapevine that he'd joined the Australian Army and fought in the Vietnam War. He actually became a decorated hero down under."

"Did your mum tell you all this?"

"Not when I was young, I didn't actually learn the whole truth until I was thirty years old as it all was kept from me ... it was strictly taboo. When I was two, my mum married Swaine and I always thought that he was my dad. However, he and my mum split up and, when I was nine, Mum married Proctor. He wasn't a nice person and, one day, when he was in one of his nasty moods, he said, 'Never mind about me not being your dad ... neither is Swaine!' I was absolutely gutted.

"Yeah ... I can imagine you were."

"Like I mentioned earlier, I didn't learn the truth about my real dad until I was thirty years old. He came over from Australia and contacted me and said he wanted to meet up with me in Burnley. This is when my mum realised she had to tell me the truth. I arranged to meet my dad in the Miner's Club and we had a right piss up and ended up three sheets to the wind. He told me that, due to his fighting in Vietnam for the Australian Army, it had scarred him for life. The next day he asked me if he could borrow twenty pounds. I haven't seen hide or hair of him since!"

"So I guess that would have upset you ... and I'm not talking about the twenty pounds?"

"Well it did at first but, I had no option but to get on with my life. Consequently, I was born Stuart Gaughan, but at the age of two my name was changed to Swaine and then, at the age of nine, it was changed to Proctor."

"Did this confuse you at all?"

"I can't say it confused me, but it certainly nattered me."

"Yeah, I can understand that."

"Anyway, I made a conscious decision and I recently changed my name back to my birth name, Gaughan."

"Oh I didn't know that ... I still call you Procky."

"That's alright Tas ... up until now I haven't told a living soul. I just did it for me as I want to leave this world with the same name as I came into it."

"Good on you Procky ... oops, sorry about that."

"It's alright Tas, I don't mind as that's my poker name. Anyway, to get on with my story, when Swaine left my mum we all went to live at my grandmother's house. It was only a tiny two-bedroom terraced house in the Duke Bar area of town. There were ten of us so you can imagine how cramped it was. To add to our misery, it didn't have a bathroom or an inside toilet. Like many other houses on the block it was full of rising damp. I grew up in that house ... it was grim"

"It reminds me of my childhood days. I was always a happy child but I would hate to live under those conditions again."

"No neither would I. Anyway, my mum married Proctor and, sadly, my sisters and I became estranged. They went living with their dad and I stayed with my mum. None of us liked Proctor, but I accepted it as my mum was happy with the situation,"

"By now you were nine ... how did you go on at school?"

"To put it mildly ... I hated it. I was the joker of the pack and forever seeking attention ... I would do anything for a laugh,"

"Oh I take it you got yourself into trouble then?"

"I did that. Like I just said I would do anything for a laugh. One day when I was smoking in the school yard with another lad he dared me to light a fag in the classroom during lessons. The teacher, Mr Baines, was furious and sent me to the deputy headmaster's study. Before slinking off I placed the still lit cigarette into the top of my desk. Mr Whittaker was the most feared teacher in the school and his reputation proceeded him. His demeanour put the shudders up even the toughest student in the school. As I stood in front of him, with his strong physique towering over me, he looked fearsome. I tried to put on the bravado act but as he wielded a bamboo cane in his hand my legs began to shake."

"I know the feeling Procky .... it's scary isn't it?"

"Too bloody true it was scary and especially when he uncharacteristically betrayed his patience by gently tapping the palm of his left hand with the cane and growled at me to put my hand out."

"Were you scared?"

"Scared ... course I wer' bloody scared. But I thought to myself, 'What the 'eck ... let's get it over with.' But then .... wh-o-o-oose, the sound of the cane came crashing down with a thunderous effect onto my fingers. The sadistic bastard must have used all his strength to muster that strike. 'O-u-cch,' I squealed in agony as a nauseating pain sent a shockwave throughout my entire system. I thought that was it but he told me to hold out my hand again, again and yet again. Four times he brandished that cane onto my throbbing fingers and, by the look in his eyes, he seemed to get enjoyment from the power he held over me. I'd had the cane before but never anything like this. He then frogmarched me back to my classroom with tears rolling down my cheeks. He was happy with the outcome until we reached the classroom only to find it filled with smoke."

"After that thrashing did it deter you at all."

"No, I hated school more than ever and I just couldn't conform to their rules. Then, one day, I did something that got me expelled. Another teacher, Mr Lonsdale, was in charge and, once again, I was disrupting the class. He got very angry and threw the board duster and at me and it caught me on my left ear. I flew into a rage and went for him. To the amusement of the class we both finished up fighting on the floor and I broke his watch. The disruption created a laugh amongst my classmates and that was good for my ego, but not so good for my future. I was summoned to the headmaster's study and then had to go in front of the school governors. They'd had enough of me and I had to go. To make it worse, conditions didn't improve at home and, at the age of fifteen, I left home with nowhere to go."

"So what did you do?"

"I roughed it and lived in an old broken down car at the back of the Town Mouse Hotel close to the Swift River. I was penniless but, thankfully, one of my sisters brought me some blankets and supplied me with food every day."

"Bloody hell! How did you go on in the winter?"

"Like you can imagine ... it was bloody freezing. Anyway I put up with it for a while and then took myself off to Blackpool and bagged a job selling hot dogs near to

Blackpool Tower. I didn't get paid but instead I got to live free in a horrible broken down flat in Cleveleys."

"Were you still only fifteen?"

Yeah I was and the Social Services gradually caught up with me and, for my own safety, they placed me in a centre called Redbank. I was shifted around and actually ended up in a children's home. I eventually moved back to Burnley and got a job in an Obidoo Store, which was one of Burnley's first pound shops."

"Oh I remember it opening but, as I recall it at the time, everything was only 50p."

"Yeah, perhaps you're right. Anyway, I stayed there for a while and, at least, I had some money in my pocket. But then something happened that totally changed my life and got me on the right track."

"Good to hear Procky. And what was that?"

"Well I got a job as a rep at Stormseal Windows and my task was to knock on doors and push their products and canvas for leads. The job suited me down to the ground and came so natural to me. I got loads of leads and felt that I had found my niche. I began to earn lots of money and earned the reputation of a GOOD KNOCKER."

"So did you work there for a while?"

"Yeah I was there for six years and I would have stayed there even longer but, shortly after Jeff Brown coming into my life, Stormseal Windows went bust."

"Jeff Brown ... who's he?"

"Well, one day in Padiham whilst waiting for a bus, a car pulled up beside me and asked if I was Procky."

"I am," I replied, "and who are you?"

"I'm Jeff Brown, and I've heard a lot about you and from this day forth I want you to work for me."

"And what trade was he into?"

"He'd actually worked for Stormseal for a few years, the same as me, but in the Warrington branch."

"What, you mean to say you'd both been working at the same firm and never met?"

"Yeah that's right but, like I said, he was working at another branch. Anyway, he poached me from the Burnley branch and persuaded me to go working for him in Warrington. The Burnley branch manager, Brian Brown, kicked up an almighty fuss and tried to get me back, but, there was no chance ... it was great working for Jeff."

"The name Jeff Brown rings a bell but I can't recall where from."

"You may well recognise Jeff from television advertisements where he's flogging double glazed windows and doors. His trade name is BOGOFF MAN."

"Oh yeah, I know the man you're on about, you can't miss him ... he's really boisterous."

"Aye he does come across like that on TV but in reality he's a truly great bloke. Anyway, like I was saying, I got into his car and we've been the best of friends ever since. From that day on we've worked in different towns all over England and to this day we still work together doing what we do best... selling! To me, Jeff is my best mate and also the brother I never had."

"I'm glad it was a happy ending and now Procky, can you tell me a little on how you got interested in poker?"

"Well, I suppose my love affair with the amazing game began in 2002 when I used to watch the likes of David Devilfish Ulliot every Friday night on channel four. I was also intrigued with World champion, Daniel Negreanu. He's astonishing and has won the World Series Of Poker (WSOP) six times and the World Poker Tour (WPT) championship title twice."

"That's incredible ... winning so many titles and each one has thousands of entrants. It boggles the mind how anybody can do that."

"Yeah, that's what I think as well. It intrigues me how he can almost read his opponents' starting hands. It's as though he's looking through a magic mirror."

"Aye, he's certainly got some kind of gift. Whilst we're on the subject ... you've been playing for nearly twenty years ... right?"

"Yeah, at first I started to play online and then I started reading lots of books about poker. I simply loved every aspect of the game."

Ha ha, it appears to me that everybody loves this remarkable game."

"You're right there Tas ... it is magical. Anyway, I realised that online wasn't for me and I started to go to different casinos and any home games I could. Over the years I have made some great friends at poker and had some good experiences. It's a great way of socialising and meeting new friends ... I just love it!"

"That's what everybody says Procky ... it's the common denominator that brings people from all walks of life together on level terms."

"You're right there. I was once sat next to Jesse from the television series STORAGE HUNTERS and he was very friendly. Another time I sat next to Joe Beevers, a great professional poker player, and he chatted with me for hours and gave me lots of invaluable advice."

Well it seems to have paid off because I think you're a great player in your own right Procky."

"Ha ha, don't make me laugh Tas."

"I'm not kidding. I've watched you play at the Ighten Leigh Club and you've won it a few times and you're always way up there in the league. I've been playing there three years now and I've only won it once. Anyroad, have you any special memories about the game?"

"I have that! One of my memorial games is when I won a Christmas competition at the Grosvenor Casino and the prize was £2500. The very next day I booked a week's holiday and flew to Egypt, all inclusive basking in the sunshine whilst everybody back home were freezing their nuts off in a snowstorm. Then, only last year in 2019 I went to Las Vegas and won a small competition in the Excalibur Casino ... it was a fantastic feeling."

"I can imagine it was ... it certainly made your trip across the pond worthwhile."

"It did that! Reflecting back over my poker life I've had limited success without winning any major competitions. Nevertheless, I still have a dream that one day I will play in a World Series event. That is my goal ... I feel that my game is solid and that I could possibly achieve my dream."

"All I can say is I think that, overall, you've done rather well ... I'd be happy to achieve what you have. On saying that, can you give me a special hand that you think is memorable?"

"Oh yeah, my most memorable hand happened when I was competing at the Goliath. I was still at level one of the comp and I had 25000 chips in front of me. My two holding cards were pocket 5's. We were still at first level and the blinds were 25/50 and a lady raised to 200 and I was the only player to call. Much to my delight the flop was 5/5/J. We we're heads up and she raised it to 600 and once again I flat called. The turn was a 10 and, this time, she bet 2000. On this occasion I pondered for a while muttering to myself and then just called. The river card was a 6 and there was no chance of a straight flush. The lady raised to 3000 and, once again I pondered before declaring 'All In'."

"You crafty sod ... you were pondering knowing too well that you had her."

"Too true ... that's the name of the game."

"Anyroad, did she call you?"

"Yeah she did, but it's funny really. She glared at me for a full minute and then asked me if I had a five. I just smiled at her and said I had two fives. She pondered a little longer and obviously didn't believe me. To my delight she called and then turned over pocket aces. The look on her face when I showed my pocket 5's was priceless. It was just one of those unbelievable hands that happens in this fantastic game. I happily scooped up all the chips doubling my stack.... gre-eat!"

****

Procky's latest event was at the Ighten Leigh Club. He didn't only win the competition but he won the bounty as well and his total winnings were £720. Like I mentioned earlier ... he is a canny player.

CHAPTER 8 - IRISH JOHN

I first met John Hanley whilst playing at the Dugdale Arms Pub and I took to him from the start. In the poker circuit he is known as Irish John. He is a similar age to my two sons and has always treated me with an air of respect. After Steve and I became partners I rang John and arranged to go to his house to chat about the book.

"You're welcome to come now Tas" he replied in a warm Irish accent, "but I'd best let you know I'm babysitting my granddaughter."

"Oh, I don't mind ... I'll be there shortly."

On reaching his house he greeted me with a smile on his face, "Come on in Tas ... sit yourself down and make yourself comfortable."

Sure enough, a little tot was crawling about the carpet in a playful way, and she was the most pretty little girl.

"This is my gorgeous little granddaughter, Scarlet," said John proudly, "isn't she just beautiful?"

"She is that John, and she's got a beautiful name too. It sounds Irish but I believe it is of Norman French origin."

"Aye you may be right there Tas. But all I know is that it's a beautiful name and it suits my little angel to the ground."

After making a brew he began, "I was born in Dublin on Dec 9th 1969 and I had three brothers and eight sisters."

"By 'eck John, I have an idea what that was like because I had three sisters myself."

He paused for a moment before saying, "Sadly, due to poor living conditions, we lost my younger sister." She was only three months old and she died on New Years Eve. We were never able to celebrate New Year's Eve after that."

"E-eh, I'm sorry about that ... I can only imagine how you felt."

"U-um, it was awful, especially for my poor mum. But life can be cruel and we had no option but to carry on with our lives. We lived in a small house with two bedrooms and a box room so you can imagine how crowded it was. My brothers were much older than me and well established amongst their peers. They were very street wise and into all kinds of schemes and hardly ever went to school. I basically fell into the same pattern. I was forever skiving off school and used to work for a milkman or a coalman. As I got older I, along with my brothers, collected scrap, old ovens, cars, wagons or anything that could be salvaged. We never dealt with scrap yards in Dublin because they paid rock bottom rates whereas in Belfast, the rates were sky high. But we had a problem because Belfast was occupied by the British Army and they patrolled the border between us and Belfast. We knew that only minimum guards were on duty after midnight and so we would set off about 2 o'clock in the morning with a wagon load of scrap. We knew that if we got stopped we would be done for smuggling but we took the risk anyway and never got caught. A slight problem was that, after weighing in the scrap, we always got paid in sterling. We had to wait for the Foreign Exchange to open so as to change it to euros. By the time we got back to Dublin it was afternoon and too late to go to school. Hence I never did learn to read or write but, like my brothers, I became very street wise. My mother was a very poor reader and couldn't teach me and, even though my father was well educated, he was always too busy working."

"How did you feel about British soldiers occupying your country?"

"To say the least it created a lot of tension. They talk about Catholics and Protestants feuding but honestly, before the conflict, we all lived in harmony with each other. When the soldiers occupied Belfast they built high walls and huge steel gates to keep Catholics and Protestants apart. The atmosphere in Ireland totally changed and there was tension in the air at all times. To me it was as if two religions lived side by side as friends and the next day they hated each other."

"How did you get on with the soldiers?"

"Not too bad on the whole but, even though I was very young, I was well aware, as was everybody else, that I had to be careful about what I said and did. A good example is when I was in a car with one of my brothers in Belfast. It was a hot summer's day and, as we stopped at the border, he put the window down for a breath of fresh air. He'd no sooner done it than a soldier jutted a rifle into the car and interrogated us."

"U-um, I can imagine that got your back up. Anyroad, how did you get on in your younger days back in Dublin?"

"Oh even then I was always in trouble and my older brothers were forever beating me up. I loved riding horses and if I ever saw one in a farmer's field I would steal it for the day and go joy riding around the countryside ... it was great. Every time I got caught I got a good beating but it never deterred me. I gained quite a reputation in Dublin and if ever a horse was missing I got the blame and always finished up getting a beating by the farmer. One time one of my brothers heard about this and he also gave me a beating for not telling him."

"Bloomin' 'eck, that wasn't fair."

"It didn't bother me, but what did is that one of my brothers would put his thumbs in my mouth and drag my cheeks apart. I didn't mind a beating but I hated that because it seemed to shock my system and I couldn't do anything. I was only thirteen at the time and I'd threaten to get him back when I grew bigger. But he would just laugh and say it was a way of toughening me up."

****

"When I was fourteen I met a girl and I immediately thought that she was the girl for me. She was from a lot better to do region than ours. Her parents liked me at first but, once they got to know what part of Dublin I was from, they tried to discourage the girl from seeing me. Their ploy didn't work so they changed tactics. They were quite influential and got me a job in England working at a Porsche car factory, so I'd be far away and hopefully my relationship with their daughter would fizzle out. I didn't like the job and got another one on a building site and also worked evenings in a pub as a barman. I didn't drink and saved a lot of money. Every six weeks I made my way to Luton Airport and flew back to Ireland and gave my mum most of my money. I carried on seeing the girl for two years but our relationship gradually faded out."

"Ah, what a shame. Then what did you do?"

"Well I stayed in Dublin for a little while more and gradually slid into the same routine as before. I never stole from anyone as I was well aware of an unwritten law amongst the local folk. It was a law passed down by the IRA and woe betide anyone who broke it."

"U-um, that sounds serious."

"Believe you me ... it was fucking serious! If anyone got caught stealing from their neighbours they got their knee caps shot off. The IRA would put a gun at the back of the legs and shoot. You could easily spot anyone who'd been found guilty of the offence as they were permanently in wheel chairs."

"I can well imagine that put many a villain off."

"It did that. Anyway, after a few months I decided to try my luck in London, but I got into a bad crowd. They were well into drugs and would steal anything from anywhere or from anyone. I used to frequent the same pub as them but I didn't get involved in their activities ... I still felt bound by the laws back in Ireland."

"Ha ha." I laughed, "I think I would have felt that way too."

" As well as being tee-total I never ever got involved in cocaine or any other drug ... I just enjoyed a game of pool. I did odd jobs here and there and then I set up a little scheme buying and selling used cars. My little enterprise was going alright until I sold a car to a so-called friend for two-hundred pounds. But, he only had one-hundred and promised he'd pay me the remainder within a couple of weeks. Well, two weeks passed by, then four and, after six weeks, I confronted him."

"Did you get your brass?"

"No, he just laughed and told me to get lost."

"What did you do?"

"Oh it was easy 'cos I had a set of spare keys so I just went 'round to his place and took the car back. At the time I was friendly with a guy four years older than me and he too was from my home town, Dublin. He happened to have a mate who'd just been released from Strangeways Prison in Manchester. His friend was also Irish and, just a few days after being released from prison, he'd stolen some bank cards and a cheque book and he'd hidden them on a derelict building site in Manchester. Basically my new found friend asked me if I would give them both a lift back to Manchester. I foolishly agreed. But what I didn't know was that the bloke I had sold the car to had reported to the police that it had been stolen."

"Oh 'eck ... so you were actually driving a stolen car."

"Yeah, it's ironic isn't it? I genuinely thought it was my car. Well things were going alright and I pulled into a motorway gas station near to the 'Spaghetti Junction' in

Birmingham. As it happened there was a lot of IRA news in all the newspapers and on television, as Manchester had recently been bombed. Well you can imagine ... we were three men with Irish accents making our way north towards Manchester. The cashier in the petrol station got suspicious and phoned the police. The police were onto it in a crack and especially when they realised I was driving a stolen car. Unbeknown to me the police were on our trail. I dropped the two blokes off in Manchester and then made my way to my sister's house in Burnley. She had recently divorced and I'd arranged to live at her house for a little while and spend some time with my nieces and nephews. I knew she lived on Albert Street but I didn't know what number. Hence, I finished up crawling up and down the street in the middle of the night and the police arrested me outside the 110 Club. They obviously suspected I was part of an IRA plot. I was interrogated and spent four nights in custody. But it didn't bother me because I'd been detained before ... at least, they had to feed me."

"Is that how you came to live in Burnley?"

"Well, yes and no ... I did go back to Ireland now and again."

"Did you ever get into any bother in Burnley?"

"No, but I could have done because I used to make a living shoplifting at different supermarkets. I only ever pinched spirits ... whisky, brandy and gin, etc... I mostly used to target Leo's and Safeways but both of them went bust."

"Ha ha, I wonder why? Anyroad John how did you manage to do it?"

"Well, what I did was I always placed a shopping bag on the back of the trolley. Then I put lots of large Cornflake and Weetabix packets around the rim of the trolley and I placed the alcoholic bottles in between them so that they couldn't be seen. As I strolled around the shop I gradually placed the bottles into the shopping bag. As I passed through the checkout I just placed items onto the counter from the trolley. One time I thought I was going to get caught as there was a policeman stood near the exit. The floor was a little uneven and I could hear the bottles rattling. I didn't know why he was there but, as my trolley was well stacked, he apparently must have thought I had paid for them"

"So you got away with the bottles of liquor but, as you didn't drink, you obviously sold them on?"

"Oh yeah, I had a regular customer ... he was the landlord of the Lanehead Pub and I used to sell them to him for half price."

"U-um, he would've been happy at that."

"He was for sure but so was I. It's funny really because at the time I was squatting in Trafalgar Flats which were due to be demolished and I refused to move out. All the other tenants had vacated their flats and I was the only person left in the entire block. Consequently, a council official came to see me and he offered me another flat if I could obtain a reference from someone in business. I got one from the same pub landlord whom I'd been supplying with alcohol. The funny part, as it turned out, was he happened to be the brother-in-law of the councillor."

"Ha ha ... wheels within wheels working together. Anyroad, did you get your flat?"

"Yeah, it was in another block of Trafalgar Flats that were not due to be knocked down for another few months."

"I suppose that was better than nothing. Anyroad, to move on, did you ever get into any scraps in Burnley?"

"John, I've never been a fighter but I've always hated bullies. I was in the Oxford Pub one night when an old man staggered in covered in blood ... he was in a right state. Then a well known bully, John Quigley, followed him bragging about what he had just done. He was laughing and I told him he was pathetic and asked him why he would do such a thing. He just smirked and told me to mind my own business. It finished at that but as I left the pub I heard him mutter that he would have me."

242

"And did you get into a fight with him?"

"I did, but not that night. Two weeks later in the Cooperation Arms he came in. Rather than let him tackle me from behind I confronted him at the bar. He immediately tried to head butt me but I was on my guard. As his face came forward I plunged my two thumbs into his mouth, as my brother used to do to me, and I forced his cheeks wide apart. I knew how he must be feeling and that's when I head butted him. He staggered against a cigarette machine that was fixed to the wall and I just laid into him with my fists. He was a big man and I didn't fancy my chances. But, like all bullies, he was a coward and started whimpering that he'd get his brother onto me. At that point I knew he'd had enough. He never bothered me after that."

"I hope you don't mind me asking but do you find it difficult with not being able to read."

"I don't mind you asking at all. The way I look at life ... I have to go down a different path to most folks. But what I lack in literacy I make up for in being streetwise. I've never been one to follow people. I do take advice but I always use my own judgement."

"Right John you've told me some good tales. Now tell me how you met Colette."

243

"Righto, here goes. I first met Colette when she came over to Ireland for a visit with my older sister Jacqueline who was now living in Burnley. Jacqueline had four children and Colette used to babysit for her. At that point, Colette was very young and I tended to take her under my wing. Although I didn't drink I used to frequent pubs and clubs. Whilst Colette was staying with us I would take her with me. But, she used to annoy me because she would drink a sip out of someone's drink and, once she'd had one, there was no stopping her. By the end of the night she would end up pie-eyed and I had to cart her home. Outside of our house is a shelter supported by steel poles. I used to prop her up on one of the poles and then knock on the door. I then legged it so I wouldn't get the blame for her being drunk. As time went by Colette came over to Ireland a few times and we were just friends. In the meantime I was never the best looking guy amongst my mates but I always had an outgoing personality. If any of my mates fancied a girl he would ask me to go over and ask her if she would have a date with him. That was never a problem for me but, after talking to the young lady, she usually said that if he hadn't got the balls to come over himself, she wasn't interested. On odd occasions a girl would say she liked me and so I finished up taking her out."

"Ha ha ... good on you! Anyroad, back to you and Colette."

"Well, like I just told you, I came back to Burnley and got a place in one of the Trafalgar Flats'. I used to see Colette on odd occasions but we were just friends. Even though I didn't drink at the time she kind of encouraged me and so I did have a few bevvies. But I could never take the devil drink and I always ended up in trouble. After a few escapades I decided it was not for me and I now only drink tea or coffee. Our relationship was still naive and innocent. But one day I was watching sport on the television when she arrived in the pouring rain. When I opened the door she was stood there absolutely soaked to the skin. She'd walked up all the way from town just to see me. I couldn't weigh it up ... why would anyone do that for me? My heart just melted ... I saw her in a different light. From that day on we decided to become an item. At first Roger, her dad, let us go living at his house until we found a place of our own. For the next 23 years we had an on-off relationship and, during that time, we had a boy and three girls."

"How did you get into poker?"

"Well, Roger, Colette, her mum and a neighbour used to play cards every night but I was never interested."

"Were they playing poker?"

"No, they were playing queens, bridge and other games."

"So, how did you get into poker?"

"Well, we stayed in every night looking after our son, Sean and, after midnight, I loved to watch a series on television about poker. I got enthralled as I watched and listened to the commentators, and that's how my poker life began. In the following years, Colette and I spent a lot of time in Ireland. I well remember my very first competition ... it was at the Rooster Pub in Dublin. Lots of posh people arrived in flashy cars and the entrance fee was 50 Euros. The top prize was 12000 Euros and I won it. My enthusiasm for the game was now sky high."

"Is that when Colette became interested?"

"No, I think she knew how to play poker from being a little girl. When Colette first starting playing poker tournaments in Ireland each event had a 'last lady' standing prize, as apparently women were not as skilful as the men. Colette changed all this because she not only won the prize every week but she also won the league by a large margin. Colette and I decided to become a team and split the proceeds. Without a doubt we became a formidable team. We travelled all over Ireland visiting different venues. No matter which one of us won a competition we always put the proceeds into the same pot. In total I won over thirty events and Colette wasn't far behind me. At one event Colette won some cash and a genuine poker table. It was no good for her so she sold it on. We both won tickets into the Irish Open but we also sold them on. Also Colette acted as dealer in many well known events all over Ireland. She became a kind of legend on the poker scene. She'd actually been to university and I realised she was far more educated than me"

"I know that Colette is an extremely good player because I've only been on the scene a short time and, to my knowledge, she's won the local competition several times. Most Saturday evenings she goes to Bolton Casino with Darren and her dad, Roger and, to my knowledge, she's finished in first place two weeks on the trot and the following week she ended up third. That takes some beating."

"Aye John, she's a canny player ... no one had ever won it twice running before. And on the third week it looked like she was going to do it again.... all the other players were giving her some stick."

"Ha ha, I'll bet they were."

"I know it was a great feat what she did but, shortly afterwards, her dad, Roger won it on his birthday. Then, just like Colette, he won it the following week and on the third week he actually finished up in second place."

"That's amazing. I know Roger's a good player too as he's won the comp at the Ighten Leigh on a few occasions and, to my knowledge, he's finished top of the league at least once. It must run in the family because your Sean is also a great player. In six sessions at Liverpool he reached the final table five times, won it once and finished second twice."

"Aye, he's a sharp player is that lad o' mine"

"Anyroad, going back to Ireland ... it seems to me that you and Colette were both having a ball over there."

"And that we were. It seems uncanny that we eventually split up doesn't it? But what it is John, our personalities just clashed ... we were too much alike in many ways. But at least we got four children from the relationship and we parted on good terms ... that's good enough for me."

"That's a nice way of looking at it. Right, now can I ask why you never do a deal?"

"Well it's twofold really. Firstly, I used to split but, after winning so many comps, I realised that I was losing out in the long run. But, secondly I play to win. The way I see it ... if I get knocked out of a comp, then that's the position I was destined to finish in. I was once playing at Manchester Casino and I reached the last three with two well known players. It went on for quite a while and they wanted to split. When I made it clear I do not do deals they decided to take 2nd and 3rd places. That suited me. In my mind, there are two categories. If you split when you are heads up ... you are a winner. But if you win the comp outright ... you are 'the winner'."

"Ha ha ... you were definitely the winner on that occasion. Right, now can you tell me of any special hands or events that are memorable to you?"

"Oh yeah! There's one that sticks out in my mind and it wasn't one of my games ... it was an event that took place at the 'Goliath' in Coventry. I'd just recently met the new lady in my life and I was smitten. You will remember it well because you were there too Tas."

"Oh I know the one, you're on about Vicky ... it's when she won the 'Joker's Wild' and she won £3000 pounds"

"That's the one. The event didn't finish until about five o'clock in the morning but what a great atmosphere. It was so memorable to me because Vicky and I hadn't been going out with each other all that long and it was the first real weekend away together. As you know she works for 'Travel Lodge' and she booked us into a fantastic room. She's a lovely lady and we met at Bolton Casino where she played regularly. We became good friends and decided to become an item. I'm really happy with that as she is now the love of my life."

"So you met her on the poker scene?"

"Yeah I did. Like you know already she lives in Bolton and she used to go to the casino every Wednesday evening. She's well known amongst the poker elite because she's won a few comps and is a regular on the final table. Without a doubt she's a shrewd player."

"A-ah, so that's what attracted you to her?"

"Well, it did at first, but you've got to admit she's got a great personality and she's nice with it. We were just friends but she used to make me laugh. I've got to admit she grew on me, she's not just my girlfriend ... she's also my best friend."

"E-eh, that's nice to hear ... you really suit each other. And I've got to agree that it was a fantastic weekend that we spent at the Goliath."

"Oh there's another event about Vicky that springs to mind and it actually happened in your house Tas. It was when you had your house warming party and quite a few poker players turned up. We all decided to put £20 into a pot and have a quick game ... winner takes all. And like the player she is ... Vicky won it!"

"Aye that she did ... I remember it well. Finally John, just one more question ... give me a special hand that is memorable to you."

"Right ... there is one that I remember well. I was playing in Ireland and I finished heads up with a really aggressive player and he was, by far, the chip leader. I had four million chips and he had at least eight million. My two holding cards were 9/7.

I was first to go and bet 200000 ... he called.

The flop was 7/7/9 ... I couldn't believe it. I checked and he raised it to 500000 ... I flat called.

The turn was an Ace. I checked and he raised to 1.7 million ... I flat called again.

The river was a J. I paused for a while and then checked. He went All In and I called.

He put down pocket Aces with a grin on his face to give him a set. But the grin turned to a pout when I turned my cards over. He had ginger hair with a light complexion but it changed to a dark red and his eyes bulged as though they were going to explode."

"Ah well, that's poker isn't it ... pocket Aces can certainly get you into trouble."

****

Shortly after chatting with John we couldn't organise our poker game due to the Corona Virus lockdown. However, on the very first game at Ighten Leigh Club when restrictions had been lifted, both Vicky and Colette split the pot and each won £410. A few days later Vicky took first place at Bootle and won £1300. Two days later, John took the Bootle final and pocketed £2100. It goes without saying that all three are certainly good players.

CHAPTER 9 - ROGER

Roger is a Londoner and that is easily detected by his cockney accent. Due to the Corona Virus lockdown I had to communicate with him over the Phone.

"Roger ... Tas here. I want some info off you for the book."

"Yeah, righto Tas ... what do you want to know?"

"Well ... anything that's interesting, humorous or even poignant that's happened in you life."

"Aye righto Tas ... here goes. I'm from a large family of nine brothers and sisters, including a twin brother. I was born in 1945 just after the Second World War ended and my parents lived in the Isle of Dogs, East London. Luckily we lived in a large flat with five bedrooms. Including Mum and Dad there were eleven of us in one house. You can imagine Tas ... there was never a dull moment."

"I know where you're coming from Roger ... it was the same in our house."

"Like any other normal healthy boy I got up to loads of mischief, but when I was five years old I fell off a high wall and suffered serious injuries, including a perforated ear drum. Consequently, after that, I was constantly in and out of hospital for 4 years. At the age of nine I was given a lumber puncture and my condition started to improve … but the injury to my ear left me partially deaf."

"What a shame … how did you cope with it?"

"Oh I got used to it, but it did affect my schoolwork because I found it hard to hear what the teachers were saying. Still, I got by. I didn't fare very well at English and other topics but I did very well at mathematics."

"How did you fare at sports?"

"Well I was never into sports. I did play the odd game of football in the schoolyard and we used to use our coats or jerseys as goal posts."

"Eh, that brings back some happy memories."

"Anyway, I always played in goal and one time a big lad, a well known bully, came up and said he was the usual goalkeeper and he told me to fuck off! When I refused he moved forward and took a swing at me. I somehow dodged his punch, grabbed his arm, and threw him sprawling to the ground. My adrenaline was flowing and as he tried to get up, I got the strength from somewhere and fisted him hard in the face. He lay on the ground for a little while nursing a busted nose but, when he got up, he wanted to shake hands, We've been good mates ever since."

"Good on you Roger ... well done!"

"Anyway, years passed and when I left school at fifteen I had no qualifications. My brother and I were both offered an administration job at a Co-op store. I wasn't keen on the job and later when I was offered another job at a goldsmith's I eagerly took it. I worked there until the age of twenty and then became a part-time manager of a local pub, the Tooles Arms. The manager was convalescing after a major operation and he asked me to run it for him whilst he was incapacitated. I ran the pub for a year until he'd fully recovered. However, because of the experience gained, I ventured into another pub, the City Arms. But this time I was permanent."

"I take it you were still single at this time."

"Yeah I were,' but one day I happened to nip around to my mother's house and my younger sister, Patsy, was there with one of her friends. Her name was Lily, and right from the start I was smitten. To cut a long story short I asked her out and we both clicked. We courted for a few years and then I took the plunge and we got married."

"A married man now with responsibility eh Roger! Did you settle down in London?"

"Yeah we moved into a two-up, two-down house. It was a cosy little place and big enough for two of us. A strange thing was the bathroom was in the kitchen. After having a bath, we had to put a wooden board over it to use as a worktop. It was during this period that my three children, Darren, Richard, and Colette, were born."

"Were you still running the pub?"

"No, I'd given that up a while ago and I was now a long distance lorry driver. In the 'seventies' I obtained my Heavy Goods License and was now qualified to drive 'Artics' and other large wagons."

"Two boys and a girl ... a nice little family. How come you ended up in Burnley?"

"Well it's a long story but here goes. My wife's sister moved up to Burnley and bought a house on Leyland Road. However she didn't like living up north and applied to emigrate to Australia. My mother decided to buy the house off her and I did the removal on one of the wagons. Lily and I remained in London for another two years but then decided to move to Burnley. We moved into Leyland Road just a few doors away from mum. At the time Colette was only two years old and we'd only been living there a few months when she was run over by a car and sustained serious injuries including a fractured scull. It was touch and go at first and she was in hospital for six months. Thank God she responded to treatment and recovered well ... it really was a trying time for the family."

"Yeah Roger, I can imagine it was ... it must have been a very hard time for you. Whilst all this was happening had you changed jobs?"

"Aye I had but I was still long distance lorry driving. I got a job locally at a place called Burco Deans. It turned out great because, being a Londoner and knowing the capital well, I got what was called the London Run."

"Burco Deans, I know the place well ... it was on Accrington Road wasn't it, close to Rosegrove?"

"Yeah it was and it fitted in well to my schedule and lifestyle. My job kept me away from home a lot and so time spent with my family was very precious to me. In my leisure time I loved nothing more than playing card games with my wife and kids. Our favourite games were Crib, Crash and 5 card poker. Colette was always a canny player and as she got older she encouraged us to play for money. It was only pennies but she loved the thrill of it."

"Aye, I can believe that, she's still a canny player ... she's taken a few chips of me at the Ighten Leigh Club."

"Anyway, life passes quickly and before I knew it my two boys were in their twenties. Darren had gone living in Scotland and Richard had bought a house in Burnley with his girlfriend. Colette was nineteen and she was living with her boyfriend, John Hanley, in Dublin, Southern Ireland."

"John Hanley, that's Irish John isn't it?"

"That's right ... you've got it in one Tas. Anyway, my wife Lily and I decided to go on a holiday to America. Sadly on the return journey she took ill on the plane suffering from deep vein thrombosis. She never fully recovered and died just months later. She was only 48 years old."

"Oh I'm sorry to hear that ... she was only very young wasn't she?"

"U-um, she was. After that I couldn't settle in Burnley and I decided to go and live in Leicester with my brother-in-law. He had two other brothers and, along with their wives, we all went on a holiday to Malaga in Spain. One fine day we went on a coach trip and ended up in a Spanish show with flamenco dancing. After a fantastic show the leading dancer encouraged people from the audience to join them on the stage. All my companions pointed me out and I finished up making a spectacle of myself. I enjoyed it but when I got back to my seat a lady was sitting in the chair next to me. She clapped her hands and said she'd enjoyed my antics and found then really funny. She was a pleasant French lady called Danielle, and she lived in Paris. Despite her French accent she spoke very good English. We hit it off from the start and thoroughly enjoyed each other's company. We spent the rest of my holiday together and decided to keep in touch. It wasn't very long before she invited me to stay over at her place in Paris."

"U-um, aren't you the Casanova then?"

"Well I suppose you can say that. I went living in Paris for a while but I couldn't cope with the language. So we decided it would be better if we spent one week in England and one week in Paris. At first she came to England for a few weeks and I took her up Scotland to my son's house and then over to Ireland to where Colette was living with her boyfriend John. Whilst I was in Dublin, our Colette taught me how to play Texas Hold'em and she treated me to a £50 tournament at a casino. It's funny really because my very first hand that I picked up was pocket aces. I bet a lot of chips but got beat by two pair on the river."

"Ha ha … that's poker. Don't tell me … you've been addicted to the game ever since?"

"Yeah Tas … you're right there."

"Did you tour around Ireland whilst you were there?"

"Not a lot but John and Colette did drive us over the border to Belfast and, Daniel and I thoroughly enjoyed some panoramic views. However, on approaching the city, I nearly jumped out of my skin. The country roads were very narrow with thick bramble bushes on either side. It was a hot day and I put the window down to rest my arm on the door. As John slowed down I got the shock of my life when I saw a soldier lying flat down on his belly with a rifle jutting through the bushes."

"Wow … did you see that?" I blurted in a kind of panic."

"Ha ha!" John laughed heartily, "You'll see plenty of things like that around these parts."

"After visiting Belfast we stopped in Ireland for another a week and on returning to England I took Danielle and showed her the sights of Burnley."

"Ha ha! That's a good one. It's a pity you didn't take her there years back in the era of clogs and shawls, factory chimneys and cotton mills."

"Strangely enough Tas, she was fascinated by the history of the town."

"Oh that's good to know. So how did your relationship go from there?"

"Well we got on rather well for a few years but then she wanted to stay permanently in Paris. I tended to travel back and forth for a while but found the hassle too much. So we decided to call it a day but to remain friends and keep in touch by phone. Sadly, just a few years later Danielle broke her leg and never really recovered. The shock to her system was too much and within months of the accident she died. Her daughter rang me and invited me to the funeral but I wasn't able to go as I was rather ill at the time and the funeral took place within two days."

"Oh I'm sorry about that Roger ... you were on your own again."

"Yeah, I was feeling quite down and so I decided to throw myself into my work. I'd just started a new job and it was the best I'd ever had. The firm supplied cat scanners and other equipment to various hospitals. The firm also made portable scanners and this is where my expertise came to the fore. I was fully trained to deliver and set up a temporary scanner in any designated hospital. Once it was operational that was my job done.

On being notified that the scanner had been used I would pick it up and deliver it the next hospital on my list. It was the cushiest job I've ever had and the money was great. I stayed there until I retired aged 65. This is when I decided to move back to Burnley. I was lonely and wanted to be nearer my children and grandchildren."

"Is this when you took up poker seriously?"

"Aye it is. Colette and John had moved back to Burnley from Ireland with their four children and they started to play Texas Hold'em in various places. One great venue they used to go to was the Bolton Casino. They frequented the place every Saturday night and I used to tag along. Sadly, Colette and John started to drift apart but it was all so amicable. They came to the conclusion they were too much alike and decided to call it a day. Shortly after that, Colette met Darren, who was running a poker league in a Burnley Pub, the Dugdale Arms. In 2014 I started going to the Dugdale Arms and I've been committed ever since. I didn't fare very well at first but with a bit of tuition from our Colette I started to win quite a few competitions."

"I know you've won a few whilst I've been on the scene. Also, John told me about how you won twice running at Bolton Casino and came second on the third week ... that's a fantastic achievement."

"Yeah, it was great Tas ... I won £1000/£1000/£600 respectively one week after the other. And it's not all that long ago. The week after my third win the Casino had to shut down because of the Corona Virus."

"U-um, I'm not so sure about that Roger ... maybe you'd sent them into bankruptcy, ha ha!"

"Oh aye, in my dreams. Anyway Tas, the second time I won it was funny really. I'd reached the last three and one of the players was Irish John. John had a similar amount of chips to me but the third player was by far the chip leader. I was already in the money and I became a bit complacent. The blinds were sky high and every time the gentleman made a bet I went All In, even with rubbish hands, and he kept folding. Every time he folded I turned over my cards. Subsequently, he got fed up of my tactics and on going All In he called me. Luckily for me, on this occasion, I had pocket aces and I depleted his stack. On the very next hand John took him out. The script couldn't have been written better ... John and I were now heads up in the final. Now you know that John never splits."

"Yeah, I'm aware of that. But did he on this occasion?"

"No he stuck to his guns and came out with his favourite expression that he much prefers to be 'the' winner rather than 'a' winner. It turned out well for me because luck was with me and once again I came up trumps."

"Right Roger, one last question ... have you ever had a royal flush?"

"Yeah I have Tas, and the funny thing is I didn't realise I had one."

"You didn't realise you had a royal flush ... it's the hand of all hands?"

"Well, what happened was my holding cards were A/Qhearts and this is how the game went."

Daz bet 500 and all players folded around to me ... I flat called.

Flop: J/10hearts - J/clubs. Daz raised to 1000 and I flat called again.

Turn: 3/diamonds. Daz raised another 1000 ... I flat called.

River: K/hearts. Daz raised to 1000 yet again.

"I knew I'd hit a nut flush but I didn't realise it was a royal. I obviously called and won the hand but it was only when Chris, one of the players, pointed it out."

"Bloody hell Roger ... you've got a royal flush there!" he shouted out excitedly.

"So you won a few chips and the jackpot as well did you?"

"No I'm afraid not. I won the hand alright but Daz wasn't running a jackpot at the time."

"Ah, what a shame! Still, never mind Roger! There's not so many people who's achieved a royal ... it only comes around every blue moon."

"You're right there Tas. Anyway .... Cheers!"

Odds-on hitting a royal flush: .... 650000 to 1!!!

CHAPTER 10 - TIMOTHY

Timothy came around to my house and we had a chat. Like all the other characters he wanted to participate in our venture.

After a brew he began his tale. "I was born in the sixties and had two elder sisters. When I was a youngster I remember having a fight on a backstreet with a local lad. He was an avid Blackburn supporter and so was I. But I wound him up saying I was a Tottenham Hotspur fan and that Blackburn was rubbish. He flew at me in a rage with fists flying. We both finished worse for wear as I had a busted nose and he had a black eye. But we shook hands after the scuffle and became good mates thereafter."

"Ha ha, that brings back my childhood memories."

"Another scrape I got into was when a gang in our district called 'The Mill Hill Boys' got into a fight with a gang from Livesy. It caused quite a fracas but then we got chased off with the police."

"U-um, that sounds familiar as well ... I think nearly every lad has gone through something similar."

"When I was thirteen, me and four of my mates ransacked a row of terraced houses that were due to be demolished and we ripped out all the lead and copper pipes. Afterwards we split up the loot between us and I hid my share in a neighbour's garden shed. It wasn't the best of hiding places and, unknown to me, the neighbour discovered it and phoned the police. Hence, the next day the police came around to our house and questioned me about it. I told them I had been playing in my bedroom the night before and that I heard some noise from outside. I looked out of my bedroom window but all I saw was the top of two boys' heads. It was a barefaced lie but it satisfied the police. They had no evidence against me and so they let it go at that."

"Did they catch any of your mates?"

"They did but only one of them. He took the rap and didn't blab on any of us ... to him it was a 'Code Of Honour'".

****

At fifteen I bought my first motorbike, a Gilera Touring 50cc 2-stroke off three brothers. I wasn't allowed on the road so I rode it up and down back alleys and on a derelict piece of ground. It cost me 50p to tank it up with a shot of Redex, which was all my spending money. On reaching my sixteenth birthday I couldn't wait to hit the road but, when I applied for a log book, I was informed that the bike was stolen. The police confiscated my bike and the brothers refused to give me any money back. I obviously couldn't take on all three at once and so I decided to get them one at a time. This didn't happen, as they moved out of town. I did spot one of the brothers years later but I decided that too much water had gone under the bridge. However, he had his own business and he went bust. I remember thinking that he deserved it."

"Yeah, as the saying goes ... what goes around comes around."

"Shortly after that I met the mother of my children. We were together for six years and then split up. It was my fault because I was a ladies' man. I wanted a fun girl but not the responsibility. I later in life became a taxi driver and that's how I met the love of my life. I got married at fifty."

"Oh that's only young ... I was seventy seven when I married my second wife."

"Blimey, that's telling me in' it? Anyway, back to when I was younger. In the eighties I got sentenced to two months in Strangeways Prison for non-payment of fines. My cell mate was an ex-soldier who had served in Northern Ireland. One night he came up with a plan on how to rob a bank. I didn't take him on but, after I got released from prison, I came up with an idea of my own."

"Don't tell me you went into the Bonnie and Clyde business."

"In one word John ... yes. But not in the same way."

"Oh, this is going to be interesting."

"Well, what it is. Back in the eighties, cash machines were designed differently than nowadays. Just like today's night safes they had a type of drawer with a huge letterbox. Once you had registered your pin number, money would drop down a steel chute into a chamber and the drawer could be opened to retrieve the cash."

"That's right, I remember them being like that. But I still don't see how you could steal cash from the bank."

"Ah well, that's when my little plan came into action. In order to test my theory I first of all drew out some money legitimately. I then placed my hand into the machine and felt around and realised there was ample room to carry out my plan. I returned to the machine few days later around tea time when it was quiet, equipped with some wide duct tape and a pair of scissors. I placed my hand inside and fixed the duct tape from wall to wall and sealed it so as to catch any cash dropping from above. I then walked away and waited in the shadows until at least six people had tried to obtain some money. When it was quiet I made my way back to the machine and slit the duct tape with a Stanley knife. To my amazement, about £700 pounds dropped down into the chamber. I scooped it up and was away from there like Jack Flash."

"Wow, I don't believe it ... it was so easy."

"John, as God is my witness, that's exactly what happened. And not only that ... I did it again to five other cash machines in Blackburn. I never went back to the same machine twice. I even kept a little notebook with the names of the ones I'd visited."

"So you did six machines in total?"

"No, that was just the beginning. Before I'd finished my campaign I'd pinched cash from banks in Manchester, Preston and Liverpool. I was rolling in it. I bought designer clothes and I traded in my car for a brand new Audi Quatro 3.2 twin turbo. It cost a fortune to tank it up but money was no object."

"You say you finished your campaign. Was that because you realised you would eventually get caught?"

"In a way .... yes. And the reason for that is because I noticed police posters on every bank warning folk of what was going on. Also, they'd started to insert cameras above every machine."

"So that put an end to your life of crime?

"No, not really ... I'd got used to the good life and so I came up with more scams.

"Wow ... let's hear them."

"Well, the next project I set up was an insurance scam. It was before the age of computers and, as all insurance companies were totally independent of each other, I could ring each firm separately. Hence, I used to insure my car with more than one company. My favourite scheme was on a blind bend. On the insurance claim form I always stated that a dry stone wall had collapsed and there was debris on the road. When I hit it the steering wheel had spun out of my hand causing me to crash. In order to make my scam work I claimed off one firm and always bought the car back. If I didn't then the insurance company would have the vehicle towed away and I wouldn't have been able to claim from another company."

"And you got away with it. What about all the cross checking?"

"Like I said, back then, it wasn't the age of computers and insurance firms couldn't keep in touch as they do nowadays. I got away with it on numerous occasions."

"Right ... I believe you. Anyroad, you said more scams ... tell me more!"

"Well, my next dodge was tax discs. By now computers were on the scene and by using a computer programme called 'Paint Shop' I could easily change the date on my tax disc. I simply scanned it and placed it on my computer. It was then simple to delete the date and replace it with another one. The only snag was that the ink wasn't of good quality and the sun would fade it very quickly. Hence, I had to replace the disc every other week."

"Replace the disc?   Ha ha, you'd have been replaced if the police had caught up with you ... replaced back into Strangeways."

"Oh I haven't finished yet. I was taxi driving at the time and, going back to insurance scams, I used to forge my own documents. It was quite complicated and, in order to do it, I had to scan the internet to find the correct fonts. Sometimes, on the back of documents, it was written in a foreign language. No matter, I scanned that as well. I always kept my 'Certificate of Insurance' in the car in case I was stopped. I was actually pulled over on two occasions but, on showing him my forged certificate the officer just gave me a 'producer slip' and let it go at that. Once I'd produced my MOT and driving license I was in the clear. Back then, the police couldn't cross check with Swansea like the can nowadays."

"Is that it Tim or is there more?"

"Yeah, there is something else. I used to use Red diesel in my car when I was running my taxi service ... it was less than half price of ordinary diesel."

"Red diesel ... what's that?"

"Well it's an ordinary diesel to which the petroleum companies have added a dye to colour it red. It's designed to be used for purposes of agriculture, horticulture or forestry only. It is strictly against the law to use it in ordinary vehicles."

"By 'eck Tim, you certainly got up to some scams."

"Aye, but it's a long way behind me ... I'm all legal and above board nowadays."

"Well, all I can say is, it's a good job that you can't be prosecuted today due to the 'Statute of Limitations Act'."

"Oh, I'm aware of that law where it states that no one can be prosecuted for certain crimes after six years has passed."

"It's just as well Tim, because they'd lock you up and throw away the key ... ha ha!"

You can laugh John, but when I tell you what my job is now you may find it funny."

"Go on then Tim ... shock me!"

"Well, I work for a 'Data Collecting agency' and my job is to investigate people who are stealing gas and electric."

"Oh I know a way of stealing gas. By uncoupling the metre and turning it around it makes the clock go backwards. But if you do it you've got to make sure to turn it back so the timing can catch up on itself before the next metre reading comes around."

"Oh so you know the scam do you ... have you done it."

"No, but it did cross my mind. The reason I never did it is because I heard about one bloke doing it in the Burnley

Wood area of town and it caused a terrific explosion and people were hurt. It was a gable end terraced house and the whole of the gable completely collapsed. The house and the one next door had to be re-built. Any road ... is gas stealing still going on?"

"It is ... but I feel sorry for some of the poor blighters because they're living from hand to mouth in atrocious conditions. I always think of my poor dad because he used to do it."

****

After noting all of his scams I then asked him how he came onto the poker scene.

"Well, I've always enjoyed a game of cards and I used to play regularly with my dad but I only started playing poker a few years ago. I went to a charity shop to check out the electrics and it turned out to be the one that Steve Wood set up to care for stray dogs. Whilst I was down in the cellar, checking the electricity, I came across a boxful of gaming chips and I asked Steve what they were for. He enlightened me that they were poker chips and he was a member of Reed & Simonstone Constitutional Club and that he played there every Friday night. I went along for a session and I've been hooked on the game ever since. I loved the game and also the social aspect of it. From there I got to know about Darren running a comp every Thursday night in the Dugdale Arms and I've hardly missed a game since ... I just love it!"

"Ha ha, it certainly is addictive. Anyroad, just one more question ... can you tell me of a special hand that sticks in your mind?"

"Oh, can I? I had pocket K's and the blinds were 1000/2000. The bet pre flop was 1000. Three players folded and the flop was 10/J/K. I was first go and bet 2000. Three others folded leaving me heads up with a guy and he called. The turn card was Q ... I checked and he bet 3000 ... I flat called. The river was a 7. I was aware that he may have an ace or a nine so I checked again. Now this particular player was well known for bluffing and betting massive on the river. He raised the bet to 10000. I pondered for ages ... the thought of folding my set of K's just creased me. I was about to call but something deep down told me not to do it. I pondered a little longer and decided to fold. What a relief ... he turned over pocket aces!"

"Ha ha! As the song goes, 'Know when to hold 'em ... know when to fold 'em!'"

****

A few days after our talk I was on the same table as Tim and he dropped a right clanger. The pot for a straight flush was £240 and Tim's holding cards were 8/9 of diamonds. Prior to the flop he was heads up against Chris, a regular player and there were about 2000 chips in the pot. The flop was 7/10 of diamonds and J of clubs giving him a straight. Chris was first to act and he raised it to 2000. Instead of flat calling, Tim re-raised it to 10000 making it obvious that he had a good hand.

"No way!" Chris reacted immediately ... you've hit a straight haven't you?"

As Chris folded his cards Tim realised exactly what he had done. "Oh blimey!" he grunted. "How stupid can I be ... I never gave myself a chance to hit a straight flush!"

Out of curiosity he asked the dealer if he would complete the deal to see how the cards would have unfolded. Sure enough the river card turned out to be six of diamonds.

"Ar-rgh no, I would have hit my straight flush!" he moaned. "Thats £240 down the drain."

It was just one of those things to put down to experience.

CHAPTER 11 - SUNNY

I'd just recently arrived from Tasmania and it was on my first game at the Dugdale Arms that I met Sunny, a young Pakistani gentleman and he was a gentleman in every sense of the word. He had a quiet pleasant demeanour about him and I liked him from the word go. The name Sunny suited him to the ground, as he had a very sunny disposition. He was on the same table as me and, win or lose, he always had a bright smile on his face. At the break he introduced himself to me and he was intrigued when I told him I was living in Tasmania. After that meeting, every time I was on the same table as him, he always laughed gleefully and said his luck was in, as I was his lucky charm.

"Ha ha," I laughed, "I've never been called a lucky charm before."

"But it's true John, I'm not joking. When you are on the same table as me, I always seem to build up a stack of chips and when I get moved to another table my stack seems to dwindle down."

"All I can say Sunny is that I could do with some of the luck rubbing back onto me."

He always played every Thursday evenings at the Dugdale and often played Fridays at the Read Club. One time at Read I had pocket Jacks and the flop was 9/5/J. Four players including Sunny bet three thousand and I called. The next card was a K. Two players went All In. Sunny folded and I went All In as well. The River card was a 2. Luckily I won the hand as one of the players had a set of 9's and the other had a set of 5's. Joyfully, as I had a set of Jacks, I scooped up a massive pot.

"Oh 'eck said Sunny, "I should have kept betting, I finished up with a flush and would have taken you all out. Anyway, good luck to you John!"

"Thanks Sunny ... it looks like my luck has bounced off you this time."

"Well, that's the way it goes ... it couldn't have happened to a nicer fella!" he laughed.

That particular game happened in November and I was due to fly back to Tasmania two days later and wouldn't be back until the following April. I actually arrived back in Manchester on my 78th birthday and the following evening I made my way to the Dugdale. Sunny happened to be stood outside with some other players and as I passed him he gave me a real good hearty greeting.

"John, you're back ... nice to see you again my friend." It was such a hearty greeting you'd have thought we'd been friends since our childhood days. Things carried on in a similar vein and when November came around I, once again, had to make my way back to Scottsdale in Tasmania. I returned the following April, but on this occasion I was home for good as I had just sold my Tasmanian home. On Thursday evening I eagerly made my way to the Dugdale Arms and looked forward to a friendly game. But, on seeing Sunny I was shocked as it was obvious to me that he was very ill. His bright, shiny complexion was now gaunt and his eyes looked weary.

"Hiya Sunny ... are you all right ... you don't look very well."

All the other players knew about his prognosis but I hadn't been forewarned and was just concerned.

Sunny could see my concern and he tried to put me at ease, "Not to worry John, I'll be all right, you'll see ... especially now that my lucky charm is back."

As I was a retired staff nurse I realised the seriousness of his illness and also his ploy to be kind to me.

Sadly, Sunny died a few weeks later and all the club players went into a state of sadness. A function was put on by his family in the club and many poker players turned out to show their respect for Sunny. His mother, brother's, and his uncles, Freddy and John Nawab, were all in attendance saying goodbye to one of life's gentlemen.

CHAPTER 12 - THE GAME

Finally, after months of shutdown due to Covid, the day of reckoning arrived and it took place at my house. Daz organised the game and the format was a freeze-out, starting with 15000 chips. To add interest the buy in was £20, creating a £200 pot for the winner, but the main focus was on the game itself. Big Pete and Vicki came along to give support and watch the outcome. To give the game more authenticity, Daz and Vicki shared the task of dealing.

The blinds started at 100/200 and they went up every 10 minutes. Consequently it didn't take long for chips to deplete if you were not winning any hands. This was especially so as Andrew kept to his game plan of betting blind and going All In. Steve started off well by winning the first two hands almost doubling his chips. The first few hands were huge and Andrew's luck was in ... by the time the blinds went up he and Steve had mountains of chips in front of them. Consequently, all the other players' chips were depleting rapidly. For some it called for emergency measures.

In my mind I expected Procky to fare well in the comp as he is a very shrewd and canny player. However, to my surprise, he was the first casualty. Due to big losses he only had about 4000 chips left and he went All In with K/J and was taken out by Tim whose holding cards were A/Q.

Irish John had just taken a big hit against Steve and was in a 'do it or die' situation. He also went All In with pocket Queens and followed the same fate as Procky.

The third player to bow out was James. By now I hadn't won a hand and my chips were down to 7000. Tim bet 2000 and James followed suit. I weighed up the situation and sussed that one of them may have an ace plus hand. My holding cards were pocket sixes and so I cast caution to the wind and went for it putting in all my chips. I don't know what their hands were as both of them folded. I was happy at that as after taking the pot including the blinds my stack had increased to 11700. To my surprise my next hand was once again pocket sixes. Following the blinds James went All In with approximately 10500 chips. All the other players around to me folded and so I called. Just like I'd suspected the previous hand, James holding cards were A/K. Luckily for me he didn't hit an ace or a king and so my sixes won the pot. I now had around 25000 chips and felt that my luck was in.

The fourth victim was Luggy. He was down to 3500 chips and Andrew went All In. Luggy's holding cards were 9/6 which happens to be his favourite hand. Normally he would have called but on this occasion he didn't. Andrew threw his cards to the table revealing 9/5. Regrettably, Luggy shortly after went all in with Q/6 and was taken out by Steve with A/8. The flop was Q/4/3 but Steve hit an Ace on the River.

Andy was sat to my right and hadn't won a hand and was low on chips. He picked up 5/6 and called a 3000 bet. The flop was 4/8/J and Andrew bet 3000. Only a seven could save Andy. After pondering a while he called again. The Turn card was a two which didn't help at all. Andrew bet another 3000. Andy felt the pressure and knew his chances of hitting a seven was slight. But after taking into consideration the state of his chips he called the bet. To his relief the river card was a magical seven giving him a straight. By now he'd only a handful of chips and he bet the lot. He won the pot and happily scooped up well over 20000 chips ... he was now back in the running.

Tim sat on my left and he'd been having fluctuating fortune and his chips were fast running out ... he desperately needed a double up. Andy went All In and Tim called with a mediocre hand. Sadly Tim became the fifth victim.

By this time I felt relatively confident. I was down to the last five players and only Andrew and Steve had more chips than me. It was my deal and my two holding cards were K/Q. Once again Andrew went All In and it came around to me. I pondered for a while. I knew that he goes all in sometimes with mediocre cards and hoped that this may be one of those times. I also took into account that should I win the hand I would be chip leader. With that in mind I took the plunge and called him. His two cards were A/J and, unlucky for me, his ace carried. I was victim number six.

Roger was the next person to follow me. To be fair he didn't have much choice as his chips were now crumbling fast under the weight of the blinds. When he came up with Q/10 suited he went All In. Steve called him with pocket aces. Unfortunately for Roger the Aces carried through to the river.

Andy was now in the last three but he knew he had to try something as he was up against Andrew and Steve and both of them had a lot more chips than he had. He constantly kept getting bad holding cards and when he stared at A/8 in his hand he decided to take the plunge and went All In. Andrew declined but Steve called with A/10. Unlucky for Andy an eight didn't show. Andy was victim number eight.

It was now heads up between Andrew and Steve and both players had a mountain of chips. The chip leader position kept fluctuating as first one and then the other went All In. This went on for a while as one or the other called All In only to be declined. Finally, the deciding hand came about. Andrew went All In and Steve called. Andrew's hand was A/J and Steve's was K/10. Much to Andrew's delight, the very first card on the flop was an Ace followed by two low cards. Steve did hit a 10 on the river but it was of no use. Our eventual winner was Andrew and deservedly so. From the offset he had accumulated a mountain of chips and he used them wisely to put off his opponents. To his surprise and delight I handed him a winner's medal which I'd acquired in Tasmania. Together with the £200 prize money he was a happy man.

Taking everything into account the game turned out to be a happy event and everyone appeared to enjoy it.

All I had to do now was to write up this last chapter and get the book off to the publisher.

The very next day, much to my surprise, a huge bouquet of beautiful flowers arrived for my wife Elsina from all the poker lads thanking her for putting on a good spread ... she was absolutely delighted.

The game concluded the end of the book. Reflecting back to when Steve first approached me and encouraged me to write the book I am happy that I took up the project. I thoroughly enjoyed listening to the players' tales and antics of true life events. In the three years since I first starting playing poker I have made many new friends and it has opened a new lease in life for me. As stated previously ... it is a magical game. I look forward to the challenge of playing many more comps in the future against my fellow players. Hopefully many poker players all over the world will be able to relate to the story and enjoy it.

Printed in Great Britain
by Amazon